Marife

# UPWARD MOMENTUM

## THE VIEW FROM THE TOP EVERYONE SHOULD KNOW

FRANCIS HERRAS

WESTBOW
PRESS®
A DIVISION OF THOMAS NELSON
& ZONDERVAN

# UPWARD MOMENTUM

*The View from the Top Everyone Should Know*
**DISCOVER THE ATTITUDES OF HUMILITY TRANSFORM
AND ATTRACK SUCCESS IN YOUR LIFE!**

# ACKNOWLEDGEMENT

I am so grateful to my family, who has been my inspiration writing this book. To my beloved wife, Evelyn, and my four treasured children Mark, Michael, Aaron, and Nathan—they inspire me to keep moving forward and to put my ideas into writings. Thank you!

# CONTENTS

# INTRODUCTION

Being humble is the way up the winning stand in life. Successful individuals have a stronger tendency to brag their finances, wealth, riches and possessions. The more successful they become they showed to have a higher tendency to develop a worldview that is shaped according to stuff, things, success and accomplishments. The purpose of this book is to equip readers the attitudes of humility the secret ingredient towards success in life, to show them a perspective the view from the top that guarantees a better way of life, and show them how to build momentum to carry out their God-given purpose at work especially in life. Humility is the winning position in life!

If you are interested in learning more on moving forward in life, please get a copy of my book, *Forward Momentum: The Art of Winning In Life.* The premise of Forward Momentum is - Failure can alter your view of life. Failure has the power to create an elusive, hollow perspective framed by painful experience in the pursuit of carrying out one's purpose in life. As a result, many people felt stuck and struggle to move forward and overcome the daily grinds of life. Forward Momentum equip readers with a practical guide, wisdom and truth from the Bible so they can overcome difficult circumstances with right perspective and mind-set; to equip readers with success blueprint and winning ideas and principles to carry out their God-given purpose. Ultimately, to awaken the dreams of those who have given up hope and prompt them to move forward from failure to success according to their defined goals in life.

*Upward Momentum: The View from The Top Everyone Should Know* consists of three sections.

*Section One: The Problem—Pride.* Section one describe the problems. First it enumerates and defines the historical Seven Deadly Sins popularized by Pope Gregory the Great in the sixth century. It discussed the problems of pride in humanity as a whole but more specifically in leadership.

*Section Two: The Solution—Humility.* Section Two is composed of ten chapters that describe how the attitudes of humility can radically transform and attract success in life.

*Section Three: The Benefits—Success.* Section three consists of five chapters that show the major benefits of the attitudes of humility.

At the end of each chapter under Section 1-3 is your *Upward Momentum Action Steps* to complete. Please write your answers on a clean sheet of paper a notebook you can use and keep for yourself while you are reading this book.

You will find *Resources the Author Recommends, Free Workshop Registration Contact* and information how you and your organization can avail *Forward Momentum Care Services.*

Now let's dive in to the book.

*Humility is the winning attitude that powers to build momentum in life.* Listen to what James, the Apostle said, "***Humble*** *yourselves in the sight of the Lord, and* ***he shall lift you up***" (James 4:10 KJV, emphasis mine). This means you ***humble*** yourself before God with a repentant attitude. *Humble yourselves* means feeling insignificant in the presence of the Lord is the secret of making your life meaningfully significant. When you humble yourself before God He promised *he shall lift you up or exalt you to do your purpose in life.*

*The Bible tells us being humble is the way to promotion the winning mindset for a higher altitude in your spiritual life.* But, the goal of humility is not the upward momentum experience or being exalted, but, *you being conscious and in need of God's presence in your life.* Furthermore, this means abandoning yourself in God's presence in the spirit of repentance; acknowledging the significance of His presence in your life and the insignificance of your presence in His holy presence. At the throne room of Jesus Christ, at His feet, humbly abandoning oneself is the highest best place one can go.

The posture of humility is the key to exaltation, to the new heights in the next level of God's plan for your life here on earth. Listen to what the apostle Peter said, "***Humble*** yourselves, therefore, *under God's mighty hand,* that ***he may lift you up in due time***. Cast all your anxiety on him because *he cares for you*" (1 Peter 5:5-6 NIV, emphasis mine). It's straightforward that humbleness guarantees you are lifted up in due time. Humility creates altitude. *It is in the realization of being in need of Jesus and being insignificant in the sight of the Lord that your life becomes greatly significant in your sphere of influence may it be at home, work, church or business.*

Having the mindset of insignificant in God's sight doesn't mean you are valueless or not valued by God. It means, in humility, you put more value and significance to who God is who created you in His image and likeness. Feeling insignificant is an attitude of humble recognition and realization that you are nothing without God but He is everything without you; this implies your total trust, dependence, superlative devotion and total submission to the God of the universe the cause of your existence.

At the feet of Jesus, is the perfect venue for abandoning oneself. This is the key to exaltation the secret to greatness and success. You can do this act of righteousness anywhere including at the comfort of your bedroom, shower, and shaving, sitting by the porch or deck or even while you are driving. Humbling yourself doesn't have to be limited or subjected to geographical location. You can humble yourself before God your Creator anywhere anytime. *In Jesus' throne room nothing is more significant than His presence. He is the King of kings and the Lord of lords.* Everything of the earth becomes insignificant including you, your accomplishments, achievements, riches, wealth, and possessions in His presence.

When you make a decision to abandon and humble yourself in the throne room of Jesus to seek and know Him with your heart, He will show Himself to you, inwardly transform your being and clarify His original purpose for your life so you can successfully fulfill your call.

Jesus Christ at the core of your being is the secret to accomplishing greater things that causes life transformation in the lives of many people. *Our Lord Jesus reminds us that the secret to greatness is the servanthood for the good of many.* Listen to what He said. "Yet it shall not be so among you; but *whoever desires to become great among you, let him be your servant.* And whoever *desires* to be *first among you,* let him be your *slave*—just as the Son of Man did not come to be served, but to *serve,* and to *give His life* a ransom for many" (Matthew 20:26-28 NKJV, emphasis mine). According to the Master, it's okay to want for greatness. Jesus is not opposed to greatness. *Greatness is good when done His way.*

In the ears of the 21$^{st}$ century culture, Jesus words may sound countercultural in today's understanding of greatness more specifically among corporate leaders or politicians desiring entitlement of being served, recognized, and elevated always. On the other hand, *Jesus way to greatness is humble service and sincere sacrifice in advancing God's kingdom on earth in the lives of people that desperately need a Savior.* Jesus way to greatness is humility that reflects the humility and service of a slave servant to his master. *Jesus approach to greatness is service to God then service to humanity.*

**In other words, your service to God and humanity done in humility is the way up—your spiritual upward momentum for exaltation.** Humility means wanting Jesus more than everything this world can offer. This means putting Jesus, His Words, and kingdom priorities first in your life. *"God opposes the proud but gives grace to the humble"* (James 4:6 LEB). *Moses was said to be the meekest man on earth but meekness is not weakness indeed a strength that is under control.* If meekness is strength under control, humility is attitude under control.

The apostle Paul exhorts the Ephesians believers to "Be *completely humble* and gentle; be patient, bearing with one another in love" (Ephesians 4:2 NIV, emphasis mine). Our Lord Jesus reminded the disciples: "The *greatest* among you will be your *servant*. For those who exalt themselves will be humbled, and *those who humble themselves will be exalted*" (Matthew 23:11-12 NIV, emphasis mine). There should be no room for pride or any form of self-exaltation among Christ follower. *Pride is the enemy of humility.* God opposes the proud. He does not uphold them. Pride exalts self up before God and others. Pride is 'me, myself, and I and the rest of me.' Pride is a humanist way of thinking totally excluding God. Pride revolves around self. *Humility revolves around God—Jesus at the core of self.*

## The Characteristics of Humble People

Let me give you my personal acronym of the word HUMILITY that describes essential characteristics of a humble people.

## H–Humble

*Humility is humble.* Humility elevates God first, then others before self. It recognizes the need of God and importance of other people and their needs.

## U–Unstoppable

*Humility is unstoppable.* A totally submitted individual to Jesus is unstoppable because the power of God works and flows naturally in his or her life. Nothing can stop God's power at work in the life of a humble person in accomplishing his purpose.

## M–Motivate

*Humility motivates and captivates others.* Pride drives people away. Humility inspire, pride infect. Humility exalts, a pride demotes. Humble people are highly motivated by the humility of Christ. Unmotivated people lacks energy, motivated people are enthusiastic people.

## I–Identify

*Humility identify to the needs of the surrounding people.* They ask, "What would Jesus do if he is in my place confronted with various people's need?"

## L–Learned

*Humility is characterized by learning.* Humble people are informed with kingdom knowledge. They are highly committed in terms of its priorities and agenda. They seek God first to put others first and seek to understand their needs.

## I–Inspire

*Humble people inspire other people.* Their humility is an inspiration to others. Their point of view is founded in Christ the real source of their inspiration. They run their lives under the anointing and inspiration of the Holy Spirit to inspire people.

## T–Truthful

*Humility is founded in God's truth* which expresses itself in a truthful, authentic lifestyle, speech and mindset. True humility embraces the humility of Jesus Christ described in Philippians chapter 2. Humility evokes the spirit of truthfulness in every facet of one's life.

## Y–Yielded

*Humility is yielded to the sovereign will of God* believing everything works together for good to those who love God and called according to His purpose. Humility is totally yielded to God's presence, protection and provisions.

### The Various Definitions and Views of Humility

My goal in this section is to show you how different religious group view humility not so much on the theological and cultural perspective. Hopefully, this will give you perspectives to aid you in your journey in the path of humility.

### *Humility in Ethics and Theology*

"In *ethics*, freedom from pride and arrogance; humbleness of mind; a modest estimate of one's own worth. In *theology*, humility consists in lowliness of mind; a deep sense of one's own unworthiness in the sight of God, self-abasement, penitence for sin, and submission to the divine will."[1]

## Humility in Religion, Non-religion and Philosophy

"Humility is the quality of being humble. In a *religious context* this can mean a recognition of self in relation to God or deities, and submission to said deity as a member of that religion.[2] [3] *Outside of a religious context*, humility is defined as the self-restraint from excessive vanity, and can possess moral and/or ethical dimensions."[4] [5]

As a sign of genuine religion (Mic 6:8) humility is necessary to enter God's kingdom (Matt 5:3 ; 18:1-4) or to be great in it (Matt 20:26-27 ; Mark 10:43-44). As the absence of self (Matt 10:38-39 ; Luke 9:23-25), it is a bankruptcy of spirit (Matt 5:3) that accrues no merit but depends solely on God's righteousness for salvation (Luke 18:9-14 Luke 18:15-17). It may involve praying (2 Chron 7:14 ; Dan 6:10 ; 9:3-20), fasting (Lev 16:29-32 ; 23:27-32 ; Ezra 8:21 Ezra 8:23 ; Psalm 35:13 ; Daniel 10:1-3 Daniel 10:12), and falling prostrate (Ezek 1:28 ; Dan 6:10 ; Rev 1:12-17) before the Lord. Since the Lord denounces hypocritical worship (Isa 58:3-7 ; Matthew 6:5-8 Matthew 6:16-18) and false humility (Colossians 2:18 Colossians 2:23),

---

[1] KJV Dictionary. "Humility". http://av1611.com/kjbp/kjv-dictionary/humility.html. Aug. 3, 2017.

[2] Herbermann et al. (Editors). "Humility", The Catholic encyclopedia, Vol 7, 1910, pp. 543-544.

[3] Herzog et al (Editors). "Humility", The Protestant theological and ecclesiastical encyclopedia, Vol 2, 1860, pp 598-599.

[4] Peterson, C., & Seligman, M. E. P. (2004). Character strengths and virtues: A handbook and classification. New York: Oxford University Press and Washington, DC: American Psychological Association. 2004.

[5] Schwarzer, Ralf (2012). Personality, Human Development, and Culture : International Perspectives on Psychological Science. Hove United Kingdom: Psychology Press. pp. 127–129. 2010.

a person's heart must match his or her posture (Isa 57:15 ; Luke 18:9-14 ; cf. Isa 6:5 ; Matt 11:29).[6]

### Humility in Judaism

In the Jewish tradition, humility is among the greatest of the virtues, as its opposite, pride, is among the worst of the vices. Moses, the greatest of men, is described as the most humble: "Now the man Moses was very meek, above all the men which were upon the face of the earth" (Numbers 12:3 KJV). Greatness and humility, in the Jewish tradition, are not incompatible. They complement one another. [7]

There is a fundamental difference between two words in Hebrew: *anivut*, "humility", and *shiflut*, "self-abasement". So different are they that Maimonides defined humility as the middle path between *shiflut* and pride.[8] Humility is not low self-regard. That is *shiflut*. Humility means that you are secure enough not to need to be reassured by others. It means that you don't feel you have to prove yourself by showing that you are cleverer, smarter, more gifted or successful than others. You are secure because you live in God's love. He has faith in you even if you do not. You do not need to compare yourself to others. You have your task, they have theirs, and that leads you to co-operate, not compete. This means that you can see other people and value them for what they are. They are not just a series of mirrors at which you look only to see your own reflection. Secure in yourself you can value others. Confident in your identity you can value the people not

---

[6] Parsons, Greg W. "Humility."1996, https://www.biblestudytools.com/dictionaries/bakers-evangelical-dictionary/humility.html. December 18, 2017.

[7] Jacobs, Louis. "Humility in Judaism." 2002-2017. https://www.myjewishlearning.com/article/humility-in-judaism/. Dec. 18, 2017.

[8] Maimonides, *Eight Chapters*, ch. 4; *Commentary* to Avot, 4:4. In *Hilkhot Teshuvah* 9:1, he defines *shiflut* as the opposite of *malkhut*, sovereignty.

like you. Humility is the self turned outward. It is the understanding that "It's not about you."[9]

## *Humility in Christianity*

Biblical humility is grounded in the character of God. The Father stoops down to help the poor and needy (Psalm 113:4-9 ; 138:6-7); the incarnate Son exhibits humility from the manger to the cross (Matt 11:29 ; Acts 8:32-33 ; Php 2:5-8). The dual usage of "meek" (Gk. praus [prau?"]) and "humble (tapeinos [tapeinov"] "low") in heart" in Matthew 11:29 emphasizes Christ's humility before humankind, whom he came to serve (Matt 20:28 ; Mark 10:45 ; Luke 22:27) and his submission before God. Humility and meekness are often inseparable (2 Col 10:1 ; Eph 4:2 ; Col 3:12).[10]

Jonathan Edwards said, "We must view humility as one of the most essential things that characterizes true Christianity."[11]

Andrew Murray describes humility this way, "Christ is the humility of God embodied in human nature; the Eternal Love humbling itself, clothing itself in the garb of meekness and gentleness, to win and serve and save us."[12]

Mark Altrogge, Senior Pastor, Sovereign Grace Church of Indiana, PA offers 4 Reasons to Pursue Humility. [13]

---

[9] Sacks, Jonathan. "The Greatness of Humility (Shoftim 5776)." Sept. 5, 2016. http://rabbisacks.org/greatness-humility-shoftim-5776/#_ftn2. Dec. 18, 2017.

[10] Parsons, Greg W. "Humility."1996, https://www.biblestudytools.com/dictionaries/bakers-evangelical-dictionary/humility.html. December 18, 2017.

[11] Tarrants, Thomas A. "Pride and Humility" 2011, http://www.cslewisinstitute.org/Pride_and_Humility_SinglePage, Sept. 12, 2017.

[12] Andrew Murray, Humility (Old Tappan, NJ: Fleming H. Revell, nd), 17.

[13] Altrogge, Mark. "4 Reasons to Pursue Humility", www.christianity.com/christian-life/4-reasons-to-pursue-humility.html. Sept. 12, 2017.

- We can't control anything.
- We are limited in our self-knowledge.
- Pride has terrible consequences; humility brings blessing (Proverbs 18:12)
- Humility will keep us from sin.

Tim Keller explains, "Humility is a byproduct of belief in the gospel of Christ. In the gospel, we have a confidence not based in our performance but in the love of God in Christ (Rom. 3:22-24). This frees us from having to always be looking at ourselves."[14]

Vernon Grounds wrote, "It is the spontaneous recognition of the creature's absolute dependence on his Creator ..."[15] (*Zondervan Pictorial Encyclopedia of the Bible*, ed. by Merrill C. Tenney [Zondervan], 3:222).

### *Humility in Catholicism*

St. Bernard defines humility as: "A virtue by which a man knowing himself as he truly is, abases himself." These definitions coincide with that given by St. Thomas: "The virtue of humility", he says, "Consists in keeping oneself within one's own bounds, not reaching out to things above one, but submitting to one's superior" (Summa Contra Gent., bk. IV, ch. lv, tr. Rickaby).[16]

### *Humility in Islam*

"Islam is a comprehensive religion and has established humility as the foundation of all sublime moral excellence.

---

[14] Keller, Tim. "The Advent of Humility". 2008. http://www.christianitytoday.com/ct/2008/december/20.51.html. Aug. 8, 2017

[15] Cole, Steven J. "Lesson 78: True Humility" (Romans 12:3), 2012. https://bible.org/seriespage/lesson-78-true-humility-romans-123. Aug. 8, 2017.

[16] Knight, Kevin. "Humility", 2012. Catholic Encyclopedia, www.newadvent.org/cathen/07543b.htm. Aug. 8, 2017.

Its absence in any soul removes any other virtue from the believer except for the superficial qualities."[17]

"Indeed, humility increases the dignity of one endowed with it. Be humble, and Allah will exalt you." (Prophet Muhammad).[18]

"…humility is the awareness and declaration on the part of a believing person that all good qualities held by him/her is granted by God, the Glorious and Merciful, and that all praise and thanks is to Him."[19]

"The meaning of *Tawaadhu'* is that man views himself with all honesty to be so contemptible that the possibility of him having any rank does not even occur to his mind. He sees nothing but contemptibility in himself. When this degree of humility has been cultivated, no claims will be made, neither in regard to *Tawaadhu'* nor in regard to any other praiseworthy attribute. A humble man is not a person who regards himself above the act of humility he is displaying. A humble man is a person who considers himself below the act of humility he is doing."[20]

---

[17] Jawad, Huda. "Arrogance and Humility", Islamic Insights, http://www.islamicinsights.com/religion/arrogance-and-humility.html. Aug. 8, 2017.

[18] Tehrani, Ayatullah Jawad. "Humility", Islam.org. https://www.al-islam.org/living-right-way-ayatullah-jawad-tehraani/humility. Aug. 8, 2017.

[19] Jawad, Huda. "Arrogance and Humility", Islamic Insights, http://www.islamicinsights.com/religion/arrogance-and-humility.html. Aug. 8, 2017.

[20] Shaykh Muhammad Abdullah al-Gang. "Understanding the Characteristic of Humility", 2013. http://islam.ru/en/content/story/understanding-characteristic-humility. Aug. 8, 2017.

## Humility in Buddhism

"Buddhism is a religion of self-examination."[21] "Like other spiritual traditions, Buddhism sees humility as a virtue. In the Buddhist text on Maha-karuna (great compassion), humility is one of the ten sacred qualities attributed to Avalokite Bodhisattva, or Buddha of Compassion. Within that context, it appears to be a natural by-product of supreme spiritual attainments that transcends the ego, just as are the four noble states of mind -- love, compassion, sympathetic joy and equanimity."[22]

"Humility, in this context, is a characteristic that is both an essential part of the spiritual practice, and a result of it."[23]

## Humility in Hinduism[24]

Be humble, be harmless,
Have no pretension,
Be upright, forbearing;
Serve your teacher in true obedience,
Keeping the mind and body in cleanness,
Tranquil, steadfast, master of ego,
Standing apart from the things of the senses,
Free from self;
Aware of the weakness in mortal nature.
Hinduism. Bhagavad Gita 13.7-8

---

[21] Tachibana, S. (1992). The ethics of Buddhism([Facsim. ed.]. ed.). Richmond, Surrey: Curzon Press. ISBN 070070230X.
[22] Yu-His, Chen, Ph.D. "The Buddhist Perception of Humility", http://www.meaning.ca/archives/archive/art_buddhist-humility_C_Yu_Hsi.htm. Aug. 8, 2017.
[23] Tachibana, S. (1992). *The ethics of Buddhism*([Facsim. ed.]. ed.). Richmond, Surrey: Curzon Press. ISBN 070070230X.
[24] World Scripture. "Humility", https://www.unification.net/ws/theme128.htm. Aug. 8, 2017

"In the Bhagavad Gita, Lord Krishna declares humility as the foremost trait of a saint."[25]
In Hinduism humility is viewed "as virtue in the Bhagwad Gita."[26]

### *Humility in Sikhism*

Guru Nanak was the first Sikh Guru. He built the foundation of the Sikh way of life, and He represents the virtue of humility. So this could be considered the first virtue of the spiritual path. Humility is a state of being as well as a continual daily process of learning to listen, obey and act upon God's Hukam. The ten Sikh Gurus were the perfect human embodiment of the highest virtues, starting with Guru Nanak who was a masterful expression of the humility that we feel when we contemplate and experience the oneness of all. Humility is the first step on the path of liberation and Guru Nanak is the light that guides the way.[27]

"Humility is an important aspect of Sikhi. According to which we all have to bow in humility before God. Humility or Nimrata, in Punjabi are closely related words. Nimrata is a virtue that is vigorously promoted by Gurbani. The literal translation of this Punjabiword is "Humility", "Benevolence" or "Humbleness." Someone whose mind is not poisoned by the thought that he or she is better or more important than others. This is a very important quality for all humans to nurture and one that is an essential part of a Sikh's Mind Set and must accompany the Sikh at all times. The other four qualities

[25] Health Community. "What is Humility", 2010. http://hinduism.ygoy.com/2010/11/17/what-is-humility/. Aug. 8, 2017.
[26] Gupta, B. "Bhagavad Gita as Duty and Virtue Ethics." 2006. Journal of Religious Ethics, 34(3), 373-395. Sept. 13, 2017.
[27] Singh Khalsa, Sat Siri. "Guru Nanak and the Virtue of Humility." Oct. 30, 2014. http://www.grdp.co.uk/guru-nanak-and-the-virtue-of-humility/. Dec. 18, 2017.

in the arsenal are: Truth (Sat), Contentment (Santokh), Compassion (Daya) and Love (Pyar). These five qualities are essential to a Sikh and it is their duty to meditate and recite Gurbani so that these virtues become a part of their personality."[28]

"The fruit of humility is intuitive peace and pleasure. With Humility they continue to meditate on the Lord, the Treasure of excellence. The God-conscious being is steeped in humility. One whose heart is mercifully blessed with abiding humility. Sikhism deal Humility as begging bowl before the god," Guru Nanak, First Guru Of Sikhism said,"Listening and believing with love and humility in your mind cleanse yourself with the Name, at the sacred shrine deep within." (Page 4,Guru Granth Sahib)[29]

### Humility in Taoism

"Humility is an important quality for a Taoist to cultivate, because when one is too proud, it invites unnecessary contention. The classical Taoists were often thought of as fools. They felt it better to be overlooked and dismissed than to receive too much attention. A metaphor used by Deng Ming-Dao shows the value in humility: The strong are conscripted, the beautiful are subjugated, and the average are left to live their lives as they choose."

It is listed among the attributes of the sage in chapter 22 of the Tao Te Ching (Dao de jing):

"Not showing off his deeds, hence [the sage] is meritorious.

Not boasting of himself, hence he leads.

---

[28] Sahib, Granth Guru. "Guru Granth Sahib on Humility", 2012. Sikhi Wiki Encylomedia of the Silkhs, http://www.sikhiwiki.org/index.php/Guru_Granth_Sahib_on_humility. Sept. 13, 2017.
[29] Ibid, Sahib, Granth Guru. 2012.

Because he is not contentious,

Hence no one under heaven can contend with him."

-- from chapter 22, E. Chen (tr.)[30]

The one common denominator of these different perspectives from the above groups is that *humility is a virtue or quality essential to grow and develop in life.* But more importantly *humility is an attitude that reflects as one of the most essential things that characterizes a humble person.*

Humility is a stand of absolute dependence on his Creator that cures one's pride of independence from God. Humility is an attitude that brings deliverance from self-centered life to others and God centered lifestyle that has the power to transform one's life from nothing to something and from failure to success. In short, humility is an essential quality to build your spiritual upward momentum.

---

[30] Tao Manor Articles Library. "Humility", http://taomanor.org/humility.html. Sept. 13, 2017.

# SECTION ONE

## THE PROBLEM – PRIDE

# CHAPTER 1

# The Seven Deadly Sins

It was Pope Gregory the Great who popularized the teaching of the seven deadly sins in the sixth century, influenced by Evagrius, a fourth-century monk. Gregory calls them the seven "capital" sins and describes these sins as the leaders of wicked armies.[31]

The order and the idea of the seven deadly sins that Gregory popularized are not explicitly discussed in the Bible, but the seven sins are mentioned in the Bible. There is a strong possibility that Gregory used this approach to teach principles from the Word of God drawn from Proverbs 6:16–19. Today, the notion of the seven deadly sins has been recognized in society's belief and literature, more specifically within Catholic theology.

Here is the list of the seven deadly sins; according to the standard list. They are pride, greed, lust, envy, gluttony, wrath, and sloth.[32] These seven deadly sins are associated with pride as the father of sins.

## 1. Pride

> *Pride* goes before destruction, and haughtiness before a fall. (Proverbs 16:18 NLT; emphasis mine)

---

[31] D. L. Jeffrey, *A Dictionary of Biblical Tradition in English Literature* (Grand Rapids: William B. Eerdmans Publishing, 1992), 699.

[32] Thomas Aquinas, *Summa Theologica (All Complete & Unabridged 3 Parts + Supplement & Appendix + interactive links and annotations)*, 2013, e-artnow. https://books.google.ca/books?id=YiJCBAAAQBAJ&redir_esc=y.

*Francis Herras*

Pride is the first cosmic sin committed and the root of every sin. The *world* operates from a sense of pride according to the apostle John: "For *everything in the world*—the lust of the flesh, the lust of the eyes, and the pride of life—comes not from the Father but from the world" (1 John 2:16 NIV; emphasis mine).

Here is a classic definition of pride in moral theology, quoted from Father Dominic Prummer's *Handbook of Moral Theology.*

> Pride is "an inordinate desire for one's own excellence." Pride is said to be "complete" when a person is so filled with it that he refuses to subject his intellect and will to God, and to obey His commandments. Such a person has contempt for God and those who represent Him. In a sense, a person with complete pride makes himself a god.
>
> However, pride may also be incomplete: Where a person does not reject God or his superiors; rather, he simply thinks of himself too highly.
>
> Associated with pride is "vainglory," whereby a person has an inordinate desire to manifest his own excellence and to receive praise. Of course, every person should be proud of accomplishments and be thankful to God for the ability to perform well. However, such a disposition differs from the person on "an ego trip" who is motivated to do something simply for future praise and recognition, or always has to talk about "I did this" and "I did that" to impress people and receive their praise.
>
> Pride is a very dangerous vice, as St. Thomas noted, because a person is so susceptible to it due to the woundedness of original sin. It can easily creep into our lives, grow quickly without recognition, and take hold, infecting all that we do. St. John Vianney taught, "Pride makes us hate our equals because they are our equals; our inferiors from the fear that they may equal us; our superiors because they are

2

above us." Spiritual remedies for pride include regular and thorough self-examination, the practice of humility and meditation on Christ's humility and service.[33]

## 2. Greed

> Then the Lord said to him, "You Pharisees are so careful to clean the outside of the cup and the dish, but inside you are filthy—full of *greed* and wickedness! (Luke 11:39 NLT; emphasis mine)

*Merriam-Webster's Dictionary* defines *greed* as "a selfish and excessive desire for more of something (such as money) than is needed." From a Christian perspective, the core definition of greed is the obsession with accumulating material goods.[34] This means a greedy person values material things more than he or she values God or people. The greedy person's heart is deeply consumed with a want for more. The motivation of greed is to acquire more things regardless of cost.

Greed is like a wildfire that burns the forest. One characteristic of fire is it burns whatever it touches. The more the fire is fed, the more it consumes

Fire can never be satisfied, and so as with greed. A greedy person will do anything to get more and accumulate more regardless of its damaging outcomes to other people.

Biblical commentator John Ritenbaugh describes it as a "ruthless self-seeking, and an arrogant assumption that others and things exist for one's own benefit." This word is also found in the writing of both Plato and Aristotle, and is strictly defined as "the insatiable desire to have what rightfully belongs to others."[35]

New Testament Greek scholar William Barclay describes *pleonexia*

---

[33] Fr. William Sauders, "What are Capital Sins?," 2003, accessed September 18, 2017, http://www.catholiceducation.org/en/culture/catholic-contributions/what-are-capital-sins.html.

[34] "A Christian Definition of Greed," Access Jesus, December 6, 2015, accessed September 23, 2017, http://access-jesus.com/definition-of-greed-html.

[35] Hugh Whelchel, "What is Greed?," January 14, 2013, accessed September 23, 2017, https://tifwe.org/what-is-greed.

as an "accursed love of having," which "will pursue its own interests with complete disregard for the rights of others, and even for the considerations of common humanity." He labels it an aggressive vice that operates in three spheres of life:

- In the material sphere it involves "grasping at money and goods, regardless of honor and honesty."
- In the ethical sphere it is "the ambition which tramples on others to gain something which is not properly meant for it."
- In the moral sphere, it is "the unbridled lust which takes its pleasure where it has no right to take."[36]

Hugh Whelchel, executive director of the Institute for Faith, Work, and Economics and author of *How Then Should We Work?: Rediscovering the Biblical Doctrine of Work*, argues that "there is an important thread that runs through these biblical definitions that is strongly missing from the typical definitions of greed. It is the idea that greed fosters the taking of something that is not rightfully ours."

## 3. Lust

> For everything in the world—the *lust* of the flesh, the *lust* of the eyes, and the pride of life—comes not from the Father but from the world. (1 John 2:16 NIV; emphasis mine)

Lust is intense longing. It is usually thought of as intense or unbridled sexual desire,[37] which leads to fornication, adultery, rape, bestiality, and other immoral sexual acts. However, lust could also mean simply desire in general; thus, lust for money, power, and other things are sinful. In accordance with the words of Henry Edward, the impurity of lust transforms one into "a slave of the devil."[38]

---

[36] Whelchel.

[37] *Merriam-Webster's Online Dictionary*, s.v. "lust," https://www.merriam-webster.com/dictionary/lust.

[38] Henry Edward Manning, *Sin and Its Consequences* (London, Burns and Oates, 1874).

Lust, if not managed properly, can subvert propriety.[39] German philosopher Arthur Schopenhauer wrote as follows: "Lust is the ultimate goal of almost all human endeavour, exerts an adverse influence on the most important affairs, interrupts the most serious business, sometimes for a while confuses even the greatest minds, does not hesitate with its trumpery to disrupt the negotiations of statesmen and the research of scholars, has the knack of slipping its love-letters and ringlets even into ministerial portfolios and philosophical manuscripts."[40]

Are you in this dilemma? Do you find yourself in the enemy's trap, designed to destroy your life? If you are, you must humble yourself before Jesus, repent, and ask him to deliver you from a spirit of lust.

## 4. Envy

> Do not let your heart *envy* sinners, but always be zealous for the fear of the LORD. (Proverbs 23:17 NIV; emphasis mine)

Envy is a zealous ambition to want what others have, be it a feeling, status, abilities, looks, or possessions. Envy happens between individuals, not between material objects. For example, a mansion cannot envy riches and wealth, but the person who possesses it can be envied by those who do not have it; in this case, people who don't live in a mansion, and who do not have wealth and riches will envy the emotions, the feelings, or the experiences that material things give to the one who has them. In other words, one cannot envy a Mercedes-Benz, but one could envy the possessor of the car and the emotion and perceived status that it gives. In short, envy is of the person who has charm, looks, and abilities and uses them to succeed in life. Unsuccessful individuals envy successful people because of what success gives—comfort, security, opportunities, riches, and much more. People don't envy success or objects; they envy the emotions, the feelings, and the experiences that success brings. Envy is a burning craving within; it is a yearning to have what others have, and envy could lead to

---

[39] Simon Blackburn, *Lust: The Seven Deadly Sins.* ISBN 0-19-516200-5.
[40] Blackburn, *Lust: The Seven Deadly Sins.*

the sin of covetousness, which could lead to evil or criminal acts to acquire those things that other people have.

Here are two aspects of envy to consider. First, we should consider the person, and second, we should consider what that person craving wants. The primary consideration is the person who has a feeling of discontentment or a resentful longing aroused by someone else's possessions, qualities, or luck. For example, a man could feel envious of the selected board members. The second consideration is about the action of the individual *craving* or *wanting* to have a quality, possession, or other desirable attribute belonging to someone else. For example, a woman could envy rich people who do not have to work eight hours aday. The synonyms of envy are jealousy and covetousness. If you are feeling envious, then the only solution is to humble yourself before God, repent, and renounce the spirit of envy from your mind.

## 5. Gluttony

> Do not be among drinkers of wine, among *gluttonous eaters* of their meat. (Proverbs 23:20 LEB; emphasis mine)

Gluttony is the desire to eat or consume more than you require.[41] Urban dictionary defines gluttony as the action of taking too much of something in. This means eating beyond your body's capacity to handle. It is a habit of constantly eating something more than the body requires. Gluttony is not limited to food; it could be anything such as liquor or games. The Bible shows its effect in Proverbs 23:21— "For the drunkard and the *glutton* will come to poverty, and slumber will clothe them with rags" (Proverbs 23:21 ESV; emphasis mine).

Over eating is sin. Uncontrollable eating habit is sin and has a negative impact on health.

Here are scriptures about gluttony.

> "And they shall say to the elders of his city, 'This our son
> is stubborn and rebellious; he will not obey our voice; he

---

[41] "The Seven Deadly Sins," Changing Minds, accessed October 2, 2017, http://changingminds.org/explanations/values/deadly_sins.htm.

is a ***glutton*** and a drunkard'" (Deuteronomy 21:20 KJV, emphasis mine).

"Be not among drunkards or among ***gluttonous*** eaters of meat, for the drunkard and the ***glutton*** will come to poverty, and slumber will clothe them with rags." (Proverbs 23:20-21 KJV, emphasis mine).

"A discerning son heeds instruction, but a companion of ***gluttons*** disgraces his father" (Proverbs 28:7 NIV, emphasis mine).

"The Son of Man came eating and drinking, and they say, 'Look at him! A ***glutton*** and a drunkard, a friend of tax collectors and sinners!' Yet wisdom is justified by her deeds" (Matthew 11:19 NKJV, emphasis mine).

"One of the Cretans, a prophet of their own, said, 'Cretans are always liars, evil beasts, lazy ***gluttons***'" (Titus 1:12 NKJV, emphasis mine).

Based on these passages, we make the following general observations: First, overeating is an unhealthy practice. Second, overeating is a wasteful use of resources. Third, overeating is incompatible with following God's law; therefore, gluttony is sinful. Also, the fact that "glutton" was one of the false accusations aimed at Jesus shows that gluttony was considered a sin by the Jews. Fourth, gluttony is associated with laziness, which is not pleasing to God (2 Thessalonians 3:10).[42]

## 6. Wrath

*"A soft answer will turn away **wrath**, but a word of trouble will stir **anger**. The tongue of the wise will dispense knowledge, but the mouth of fools will pour out folly"* (Proverbs 15:1-2 LEB, emphasis mine).

---

[42] Compelling Truth. "What is the sin of gluttony?" 2011-2017. https://www.compellingtruth.org/gluttony-sin.html. Oct. 2,2017

According to Strong's Hebrew and Greek Dictionary the word wrath is a primitive root; to *breathe* hard, that is, *be enraged:* - be angry (displeased).

> Wrath, when used of man, is the exhibition of an enraged sinful nature and is therefore always inexcusable (Genesis 4:5,6; 49:7; Proverbs 19:19; Job 5:2; Luke 4:28; 2 Corinthians 12:10; Galatians 5:20; Ephesians 4:31; Colossians 3:8). It is for this reason that man is forbidden to allow anger to display itself in his life. He is not to give place unto wrath (Romans 12:19), nor must he allow the sun to go down upon his wrath (Ephesians 4:26). He must not be angry with his brother (Matthew 5:22), but seek agreement with him lest the judgment that will necessarily fall upon the wrathful be meted out to him (Matthew 5:25, 26). Particularly is the manifestation of an angry spirit prohibited in the training and bringing up of a family (Ephesians 6:4; Colossians 3:19). Anger, at all times, is prohibited (Numbers 18:5; Psalms 37:8; Romans 12:19; Galatians 5:19; Ephesians 4:26; James 1:19-20).[43]

## 7. Sloth

*"Through **sloth** the roof sinks in, and through **idleness** of hands the house leaks"* (Ecclesiastes 10:18 LEB, emphasis mine).

*"**Slothfulness** casteth into a deep sleep; and an idle soul shall suffer hunger"* (Proverbs 19:15 KJV, emphasis mine).

Miriam Webster Dictionary defines sloth as indolence, spiritual apathy and inactivity. So, to be slothful means to be lazy, reluctance to work or make an effort to do the essentials of life. Slothfulness is laziness. God hates laziness.

*The seven sins enumerated are historically considered as the most fatal sins one can commit fatal enough to kill spiritual growth and progress.* Biblically,

---

[43] Orr, James, M.A., D.D. General Editor. "Wrath, (Anger)," <u>International Standard Bible Encyclopedia</u>. Public Domain, 1915.

the root cause of sins can be traced back to the fall of Lucifer when he exalts himself above God because of pride and deceived one third of the angelic host to revolt against God. Lucifer turns a host of angels into a host of devils. The sin of Lucifer was the gateway of sins into humanity the root cause of disobedience of the first human being Adam in the Garden of Eden. The Genesis account gives empirical evidence of the autonomous exercise of human free will outside the bounce of God's defined moral law in the Garden of Eden.

**ℒℒℒ**

## "The seven sins enumerated are historically considered as the most fatal sins one can commit fatal enough to kill spiritual growth and progress."

**Francis Herras**

**ℒℒℒ**

Pride was the cause of Satan's fall and banishment from heaven. Satan's desire to take over God's throne, to exalt himself above God and want to be worshipped caused his fall but one must remember that it originated from his pride (Isaiah 14:12-14). Satan's pride had caused heavenly revolt and the fall of the first couple Adam and Eve. With Satan's deceptive temptation the couple yielded to violate God's moral law not to eat the tree of knowledge of good and evil. Here we witness the transference manifestation of Satan's pride into man's free will through disobedience. Pride gives birth to pride and pride to disobedience.

*Seeing* and *hearing* is a part of man's five senses that could trigger an array of varying thoughts both negative and positive thoughts that could potentially translate into either ethical or unethical behaviors. A perfect example of the impact of seeing and hearing was Eve's experience in the Garden of Eden when she was tempted by Satan in a form of a serpent as elaborately described in Genesis chapter three. Let's have a look at it.

"Now the ***serpent*** was more crafty than any of the wild animals the Lord God had made. He said to the woman, "Did God really say, 'You must not eat from any tree in the garden'?" **[HEARING]** (Genesis 3:1 NIV, insertions and emphasis mine)

The woman said to the serpent, "We may eat fruit from the trees in the garden, but God did say, 'You must not eat fruit from the tree that is in the middle of the garden, and you must not touch it, or you will die.'" (Genesis 3:2-3 NIV)

"You will not certainly die," the serpent said to the woman. "For God knows that when you eat from it your eyes will be opened, and you will be like God, knowing good and evil" **[HEARING]** (Genesis 3:4-5 NIV, insertions mine)

*When the woman **saw** [**SEEING**] that the fruit of the tree was good for **food** [**TASTING**] and **pleasing** to the **eye**, [**PERCEPTION/LUST**] and also desirable for **gaining wisdom**, [**EMOTION/FEELING**] she took some and ate it. She also **gave** some to her husband, [**BEHAVIORS/ ACTIONS**] who was with her, and he ate it. Then the eyes of both of them were **opened**, and they **realized** they were **naked**; [**CONSECQUENCES/IMPACTS**]* so they sewed fig leaves together and made coverings for themselves." (Genesis 3:6-7 NIV, insertions and emphasis mine)

Eve's experienced:

- **Saw**– *"the fruit"*
- **Perceived**– *"the tree was good for food and pleasing to the eye"*
- **Emotions**– *"desirable for gaining wisdom"*

- **Actions**– "*she took some and ate it. She also gave some to her husband*"
- **Impacts**- *the eyes of both of them were opened, and they realized they were naked; so they sewed fig leaves together and made coverings for themselves.*"

Note that the consequences and impact of Eve's thoughts and actions leads to her and her husband's fall, banishment from the Garden and the entrance of sin that leads to moral depravity of the coming generations. Eve's actions totally violates the moral law that God put in place in the Garden for them to follow, bear in mind this disobedience before their fall. That law was, "*You are free to eat from any tree in the garden; but you must not eat from the tree of the knowledge of good and evil, for when you eat from it you will certainly die.*" (Genesis 2:15-17 NIV). God's law provides the first couple a moral guideline what they can and can't do. That law clearly gives them a well-defined limits and consequences if not followed.

In the Garden we see man's exercise of *the gift of autonomy*; but, that autonomy was exercised in disobedience to Gods' moral law that has been set and provided. Here we observed that *the exercise of autonomy in violation or in contradiction to God's law had caused the fall of man.* This tells us that *exercising autonomy doesn't mean ignoring God's moral expectations and overriding man's responsibility and obligation to follow God's moral law in today's world that does not recognize Gods' absolutes and moral standard whether it be in the context of providing a care services or passing a legislative law.* This means for *professional, patient, client or resident to follow Gods' moral limits in the exercise of autonomy* in a civilized society.

The diagram below shows the interconnectedness progressions of responses leading to commit one of the Seven Deadly Sins. Eve's experienced could happen to Christian individuals facing different evil temptations in life.

The diagram below depicts the sources, dynamics, and progression of physiological and psychological responses when one is confronted with temptations ferociously. The diagram will likewise show a very important reaction of the responder with their mind (perception), emotions (feelings), will (choice), actions (behaviors) and the impacts or effect of their response. The diagram further identifies the role of the four *primary emotions* when one is faced with temptations or challenging moral plight. The diagram elaborates more on the dynamic of the soul or psychological dimensions as the very seat of the individual's temperament.

Understanding this Interconnectedness Progression is essential to deepen one's level of spiritual awareness as follower of Christ as professional practitioner or care service provider in any setting. This could be used for a debriefing but more importantly for assessing one's personal responses in a given condition.

Let's look at the diagram to examine closely Eve's responses when she was tempted by Satan in the Garden of Eden.

## Eve's Interconnectedness Processes of Progressions

EVE'S PROCESESS PROGRESSIONS

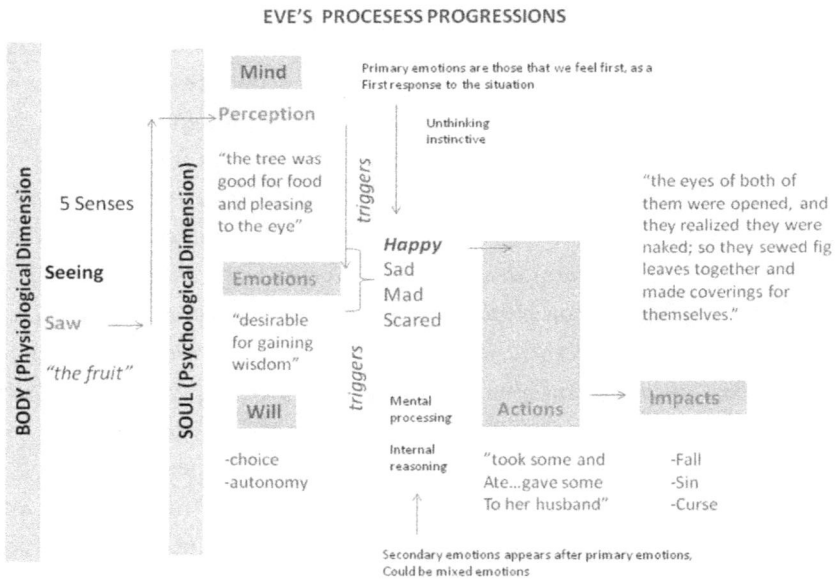

**Mind**

Primary emotions are those that we feel first, as a First response to the situation

Perception

Unthinking instinctive

"the tree was good for food and pleasing to the eye"

*triggers*

*Happy*
Sad
Mad
Scared

"the eyes of both of them were opened, and they realized they were naked; so they sewed fig leaves together and made coverings for themselves."

Emotions

"desirable for gaining wisdom"

*triggers*

Mental processing

**Actions**

**Impacts**

Will

-choice
-autonomy

Internal reasoning

"took some and Ate...gave some To her husband"

-Fall
-Sin
-Curse

Secondary emotions appears after primary emotions, Could be mixed emotions

BODY (Physiological Dimension)

5 Senses

Seeing

Saw

"the fruit"

SOUL (Psychological Dimension)

# CHAPTER 2

# The Problems of Pride

Pride has been called the sin from which other sins arise. Pride is likewise known as vanity. Pride is self-centered belief that hinders individuals to acknowledge God's grace and sovereignty.

## In Leadership

Dr. John Maxwell in his book "Sometimes You Win, Sometimes You Learn," talks about The Importance of a Spirit of Humility. He said, "Some people fail forward. Others fail and quickly spiral downward. These two types of people are very different, but how? The difference is on the inside. It's the spirit of the individual. Those who profit from adversity possess a spirit of humility and are therefore inclined to make the necessary changes needed to learn from their mistakes, failures, and losses. They stand in stark contrast to prideful people who are unwilling to allow adversity to be their teacher and as a result fail to learn."[44]

In Pride - A Leader's Greatest Problem by Dr. John C. Maxwell – as published in January 2007 Leadership Wired he shares the story of Alexander Hamilton.

> "Pull a 10-dollar bill from your pocket, and you will see the face of Alexander Hamilton on the front. By merit

---

[44] John C. Maxwell, <u>Sometimes You Win, Sometimes You Learn</u> (New York: Center Street, 2013), p. 19.

of his accomplishments, Hamilton should be one of our greatest national heroes. Consider his contributions to America:

- Revolutionary War hero
- George Washington's chief of staff by age 22
- America's first Secretary of the Treasury
- Co-author of The Federalist Papers
- Creator of the Coast Guard
- Designer of the nation's banking and finance system
- Architect of a system of tax collection to bring revenue to the U.S. Government
- Builder of the infrastructure for an industrial economy

Yet, despite displaying the greatest blend of legal, political, and financial knowledge of the founding fathers, Hamilton does not rank among the foremost heroes of our country's history. Why? Pride. Hamilton's self-importance and inability to take an insult alienated those around him and sabotaged his career. His ego literally killed him. Far too vain to patch up differences with fellow politician, Aaron Burr, Hamilton was shot and killed by Burr in a duel at the age of 49."[45]

In Mere Christianity, C. S. Lewis writes this about pride: "There is one vice of which no man in the world is free; which everyone in the world loathes when he sees it in someone else; and of which hardly any people, except Christians, ever imagined that they are guilty themselves. I have heard people admit that they are bad-tempered, or that they cannot keep their heads about girls or drink, or even that they are cowards. I do not think I have ever heard anyone who was not a Christian accuse himself of this vices. And at the same time I have very seldom met anyone, who was not a Christian, who showed the slightest mercy to it in others. There is no fault which makes a man more unpopular, and no fault which we are

---

[45] Maxwell, John C. "Pride – A Leader's Greatest Problem". 2007. http://www.stma.org/sites/stma/files/pdfs/pride_a_leaders_greatest_problem.pdf. Sept. 13, 2017.

unconscious of in ourselves. And the more we have it in ourselves the more we dislike it in others."[46]

The Bible in the Old Testament shows some of the results of pride? It led to Uzziah's downfall (2 Chron 26:16); it hardened the heart of Nebuchadnezzar (Dan 5:20); it goes before destruction (Prov 16:18); it does not seek God (Psalm 10:4); it brings disgrace (Prov 11:2); it breeds quarrels (Prov 13:10); it deceives (Jer 49:16 ; Obad 1:3); it brings low (Prov 29:23 ; Isa 2:11 ;23:9); it humbles (Isa 2:17 ; Dan 4:37).[47]

---

[46] Lewis, C. S., "Mere Christianity – Chapter 8" in *The Great Sin*, (London : Collins, 2012), 94.

[47] Elwell, Walter A. "Entry for Pride", Evangelical Dictionary of Theology, 1997. http://www.biblestudytools.com/dictionaries/bakers-evangelical-dictionary/pride. html. Sept. 13, 2017.

# SECTION TWO

# THE SOLUTION - HUMILITY

The Attitudes of Humility why it can radically
transform and Lead to Success in your Life

## CHAPTER 1

# Humility Recognizes that Everything is Given from Heaven

*"A man can receive not **one thing** unless it is granted to him from heaven!"* (John 3:27 LEB, emphasis mine)

*"Humility is not denying the power you have but admitting that the power comes through you and not from you."*[48]

   *"A person cannot receive even **one thing** unless it is given him from heaven"* (John 3:27 ESV, emphasis mine). This statement of John the Baptist, gives me, an exhilarating and liberating experience while reflecting on it. I felt something deep inside of me has been unleashed and released. I felt free inside and experienced tremendous peace the moment I believe it, prayed it, and make it my own personal declaration. I suddenly look at my life with deep reflective realization that everything I have, everything that is and has been happening in my life has been given from heaven, they are an integrated part of God's sovereign workings upon my life to grow me and make me the person He wants me to become. *I realized every single thing I have has been given from heaven! Everything has gone through God's handling of filtering approval.* There is nothing, not even *"one thing"*

---

[48] Smith, Fred. "Christian Humility", 1984. http://www.christianitytoday.com/pastors/1984/winter/84l1118.html. Sept. 18, 2017.

19

in my life including my household that is not given by God. Everything I have has been given by God who loves me and bless me in so many ways beyond my comprehension.

ჟ.ჟ.ჟ

# "I realized every single thing I have has been given from heaven! Everything has gone through God's handling of filtering approval."

**Francis Herras**

ჟ.ჟ.ჟ

This *"one thing"* is our marriage, children, work, house (s), vehicles, savings, properties, friends, money, business opportunities, including the 365 days encapsulated in the year the future he has prepared for us.

Is this how you view things as you examine your life and the blessings you've received from the day you were born? Do you recognize that everything is given from heaven? If you do that recognition or realization can only arise from the spirit of humility. You are on the right tracked to exaltation.

---

**UPWARD MOMENTUM ACTION STEPS**

Do you recognize that everything is given from heaven?

In your own words describe the spirit of humility.

How would you describe the condition of your heart?

---

# CHAPTER 2

# Humility Recognizes that All Things Were Made Through Him

*"For years, maybe, you have tried fruitlessly to exercise control over yourself, and perhaps this is still your experience; but when once you see the truth you will recognize that you are indeed powerless to do anything, but that in setting you aside altogether God has done it all. Such discovery brings human striving and self-effort to an end."(Watchman Nee)*

*"**All things** were **made through him**,* and without him was not anything made that was made" (John 1:3 NKJV, emphasis mine).

Today is your day the beginning of new things and great things in your life. *When you humble yourself before God's presence you enter into a realm that will catapult you to your purpose.*

Submission to the authority of Jesus and His Words is the secret of building your spiritual momentum your way to exaltation. Total surrender to the Lordship of Jesus Christ is your upward momentum that will radically transform the landscape of your walk with God and your relationship with other people beginning with your love ones.

⚘⚘⚘

# "When you humble yourself before God's presence you enter into a realm that will catapult you to your purpose."

**Francis Herras**

⚘⚘⚘

I urge you to make it your lifetime commitment to read the Bible book-by-book to allow Jesus speak into your heart through the pages of His infallible Words. *Jesus is the beginning of great things!* I want you to listen to what the apostle John said: *"All things were made through him, and without him was not anything made that was made"* (John 1:3 NKJV). The apostle John claims without Jesus nothing that you see in the universe is made including you. Everything was made through Jesus!

Through Jesus the whole universe existed. There was nothing made apart from Jesus. *"All things were MADE THROUGH HIM, and without him was not anything made that was made"* (John 1:3 NKJV, emphasis mine). This is the truth to learn from Jesus in terms of causing something great to happen in our personal life, meaning turning your great ideas to a concrete reality. Jesus is our perfect model in executing our purpose in life.

In this life we live, everything happens through Him, as we put our trust, and hope in Christ. Meaning, things happen in our life because Jesus allows it to happen as we prayerfully execute our desired written goals. This further means, that you and I have an important role to play in life, that is, to cause good things to happen base on our choices, decisions and actions in terms of accomplishing our vision and dreams. No one will do this for you but you. It is your responsibility to discover your destiny an essential ingredient to your personal growth, success and development in the journey of life.

◆◆◆

# "In this life we live, everything happens through Him, as we put our trust, and hope in Christ. Meaning, things happen in our life because Jesus allows it to happen as we prayerfully execute our desired written goals."

**Francis Herras**

◆◆◆

*"In him was life"* (John 1:4 NKJV)

In Jesus was life! In Jesus is life! In short, Jesus is my life and your life! His breath is in me and you, in my lungs and your lungs! You breathe the breath of life from God the day you were born. His breath in you—the breath of life! You are a vessel of God's life. You have the life of God in you that sustains you. Every day His life transforms and molds you into his image and likeness. His life is your life. In him you live and move and have your being! Jesus is your life!

*"The light shines in darkness"* (John 1:5 NKJV).

Jesus light shines in this darkened world more than 2000 years ago until now. There is no measure of darkness that can dim Jesus light. No forces of evil can overcome Jesus light. As a Christian, Jesus light is your light! His light shines in, on, and through you to lighten up your marriage, home, work and business.

His light dispels internal darkness hidden in your soul—thoughts, emotion or psychological realm. His light is the true light that purifies your mind both your conscious mind and subconscious mind. He is the light of your children and the coming generations you will not see. There is no measure of darkness that can dim the light of Jesus in you. His light will continue to shine through you in this darkened world to bear witness to the True Light that the world desperately needs to see and experience.

ʕʕʕ

# "As a Christian, Jesus light is your light! His light shines in on, and through you to lighten up your marriage, home, work and business."

**Francis Herras**

ʕʕʕ

---

### UPWARD MOMENTION ACTION STEPS

How would you interpret *all things were made through him* in your own context of life?

Reflect at your life then interpret and apply *without him (Jesus) was not anything made that was made?*

---

# CHAPTER 3

# Humility Longs For God's Presence: "One Thing Have I Asked of the Lord"

*"God is not looking for extraordinary characters as His instruments, but He is looking for humble instruments through whom He can be honored throughout the ages."*
*- A. B. Simpson*

On one occasion, just before going to sleep, I was reading a couple of chapters in the Book of Psalm to hear from God speak into my heart to find refreshment from his word. Psalm 27 resonate into my heart specifically verse four where David pours out his whole heart to God and said, *"ONE THING have I asked of the Lord, that I will seek after and that I may dwell in the house of the Lord all the days of my life, to GAZE upon the BEAUTY of the Lord and to inquire in his temple" (Psalm 27:4 KJV, emphasis mine).*

There is always that *"one thing"* that we ask of God. I totally understand King David as he pours his heart for that *"one thing"* that's consuming his heart and mind in his prayers. We have this somewhat prayer that consumes our hearts. We have blazing prayer that dominates every time we pray. This *"one thing"* sticks deep into our deepest consciousness wherever we go and whatever we do. This *"one thing"* is the cry of our being in difficult times or in times of crises in life. This *"one thing"* will always be the concluding summary of our prayers. This *"one thing"* is the short version that encapsulates the translation of our heart's cry to God. This *"one thing"* has been the source of inspiration, encouragement and direction of our lives as we forged the reality of the jungle of life; a life that will definitely brings various kinds of testing, trials and challenges to grow, mature, overcome and to move us forward.

Have you ever asked yourself what is that *"one thing"* that encapsulates your prayer; that *"one thing"* that consumes your entire being?

Allow me to share with you the *"one thing"* that drives the denomination that I am affiliated with – The Western Canadian District of the Christian Missionary Alliance. This is the pulse of our movement articulated in prayer:

> "Oh God, with all our hearts, we long for you. Come; transform me to be Christ-centered, spirit empowered, mission-focused people, multiplying disciples everywhere."[49]

> "This prayer reflects the cry of our hearts as we desire to align our will with God's in being set apart for His redemptive purpose in the world. It is our desire for our churches to be known by the love we have for each other, as we embrace the marginalized and extend hope where despair reigns; becoming places of hope and healing where everyone belongs. We want to continue to the health and vitality of our surrounding community, as we live 'mission focused' locally and send people globally. With a charging societal landscape around me, we remain flexible in responding to the moving of God's Spirit as we move creatively in planting gospel communities among ethnically and culturally diverse peoples."[50]

King David knew that one thing. He identified and proclaim it before His Creator - ***"ONE THING** have I asked of the Lord, that I will seek after and that I may dwell in the house of the Lord all the days of my life, to GAZE*

---

[49] Transform Western Canadian District of the C&MA. "Vision and Values", http://transformcma.ca/who-we-are/vision-and-values/. Sept. 28, 2017.
[50] Ibid

*upon the BEAUTY of the Lord and to inquire in his temple,"* (Psalm 27:4 KJV, emphasis mine).

If I have to summarize David's passion, it would be—***presence and purpose***! David's *"one thing"* is God's presence upon his life; to enjoy God and gaze upon his beauty; enjoying God's purpose! This is David's consuming desire. What about you? What do you desire in your heart? What are you passionate for? What is that one thing that you ask of God that sets your heart ablaze?

❦❦❦

## "David's *"one thing"* is God's presence upon his life; to enjoy God and gaze upon his beauty; enjoying God's purpose!"

**Francis Herras**

❦❦❦

I know mine. *"Oh God, please use me according to your original intent and purpose you've created me; your will be done in every aspects of my life."* This is the cry of my heart! This is the pulse of my prayer! This summarize the passion of my heart—to do God's original intent, design and purpose in my life here on earth and that I will not miss everything that he had prepared for me while I am alive.

❦❦❦

## "Oh God, please use me according to your original intent and purpose you've created me; your will be done in every aspects of my life."

**Francis Herras**

❦❦❦

I noticed that this has been the prevailing theme in my prayer life to God. Many times, I wrestle with God, and ask questions such as, "am I in the right tract, am I walking within the bounce of your purpose, am I accomplishing your purpose in what I am doing now as a clinical chaplain? These are a few of the questions that I wrestled with God in my prayers. In my case, *if I have to describe my heart's passion in two descriptive words, it would be—God's **purpose and presence*** in my current life condition. I have shed lots of tears and pour out my whole being before God on this two prevailing theme in my prayer life—a yearning want of his original intent, design and purpose for my life and the covering of his presence wherever I go as long as I lived.

What about you? What is your personal *"one thing"*? For King David, it was the presence and purpose - to enjoy God and gaze upon his beauty; to be with God, enjoying accomplishing God's purpose!

Mine is ***purpose and presence*** - a yearning desire of his original intent, design and purpose in my life and the covering of his presence wherever I go as long as I live. What about you? I want you to pause reading right now and write down your consuming "one thing." Identify them and ask Jesus why you have them. *Discover and unfold the deepest cry of your heart!* This could be the utmost passion hidden deep inside of you that need to be unleashed a gateway to find your God-given purpose of existence.

## A.  Powerful Antidote for Loneliness

The most powerful antidote for loneliness, unhappiness, and depression is ***"the joy of the Lord!"***

> *"You make known to me **the path of life**; in your presence there is <u>fullness of joy</u>; at your right hand are <u>pleasures forevermore</u>."* (Psalm 16:11 LEB, emphasis mine)

God is the author of life; he alone has the path of life. The word *"path"* means, a way or track laid for walking or made by continual treading. It could further mean, a route or course along which someone or something travels.

Here David acknowledges God's active involvement in his life. He boldly declares *"you make known to me the path of life."* This implies *a path that God has prepared for each of his children to walk*. There is a lifestyle that God want for his children.

The path of life God has made known to David; I think, in this context, is the path of life that is conscious and honor God's presence. It is a lifestyle of enjoying God's presence *"in your presence"* as David indicated. It is a lifestyle that is fully aware, mindful; enjoy God Himself in the daily activities of life where everything revolves around His presence as the whole universe revolves around Him. The Throne of Jesus is the center of the universe; it sustains the universe; give the order in the universe; and it reflects his power, wisdom, glory and majesty. The whole creation declares God's glory. It declares who God is.

ঌঌঌ

## "The Throne of Jesus is the center of the universe; it sustains the universe; give the order in the universe; and it reflects his power, wisdom, glory and majesty."

### Francis Herras

ঌঌঌ

David had discovered by revelation a path of life that revolves around God's presence. A life that is sustained preserved and protected by God Himself. A life not only acknowledges, but a life that is in total dependence on Him; a life that walks with Him; a life that honors Him in every way and everything; a life that pleases Him; a life of faith solely upon Him; a life that sees life through His eyes; a life where Jesus is at the core! In my opinion, the path of life that David was referring was the path of life revealed by God his Creator.

David understood a greater path of life which he embraced as reflected on his Psalm. *David is described as a man after God's own heart.* He was a man of God's presence. He thirsts and yearns for God's presence. The entire book of Psalm in the Bible is a product of David's intimate walk with

God that shows the relationship he had with God. He was not perfect, he intentionally made mistakes but his heart revolves around God.

*"In your presence there is fullness of joy"* (Psalm 16:11 LEB). This is a description of life where Jesus at the core, the *"fullness of joy ... pleasures forevermore."* Experiencing God is experiencing the fullness of joy. The fullness of joy only happens in the presence of God where God is the only Source of that joy. It is fullness of joy because of *the joy of the Lord.*

❧❧❧

# "Experiencing God is experiencing the fullness of joy. The joy of the Lord is the fullness of joy!"

### Francis Herras

❧❧❧

*The joy of the Lord is the fullness of joy!* The only way to experience this joy is through the Holy Spirit deposited and at work in us. This is uncontaminated pure joy fresh from the pure heart of God oozing through your life; the joy of the Lord that strengthens your being in every way. This is the real lasting joy that overcomes loneliness; the real joy that transform passionless life into passionate life; the real joy that creates godly enthusiasm a momentum that catapult one from unproductiveness to productiveness; the joy of the Lord that conquers depression or melancholic spirit and turn it into rejoicing and dancing. It is the joy that makes heaven rejoices! It is the joy that makes the entire creation rejoices! It is the joy that makes one rejoice! It is the joy that makes the church rejoices! It is the joy that sustains his children on earth! It is the joy that makes people of God glad in spite of the daily grinds of life! It is the joy that moves us forward to our destiny! The joy that energize our being to laugh, live and love and have our being! It is the joy of the Lord the source of our strength that keeps us from loneliness. It is the joy of the Lord that empowers us and moves us from status quo into greater things in the kingdom of God. It is the joy that makes the job well done!

The joy of the Lord is my fullness of joy that carries me to carry out my ultimate purpose in life. Without it life is miserable, melancholic mess.

The joy of the Lord creates divine pleasures within my soul that the world cannot give and money can't buy.

In the presence of God is *"pleasures forevermore."* David experienced godly pleasure; unexplainable pleasure oozing from the presence of God. *I think, the most powerful antidote for loneliness, unhappiness, depression is "the joy of the Lord" the real cure for emotional deficiency.*

♪.♪.♪

## "I think the most powerful antidote for loneliness, unhappiness, depression is 'the joy of the Lord' the real cure for emotional deficiency."

### Francis Herras

♪.♪.♪

This is the life that I want, and the life God desires for you here on earth; a life consume by his presence, oozes his joy and pleasure to a lonely world!

## B. The Key to Happiness

*The presence of God and the joy of the Lord is the key to real lasting happiness!* You can put a person in very fun activities or events, but he or she still will not be happy. Why? Because no fun activities or events can make anyone happy. There is no measure of money, wealth, and riches that can make one happy. Happiness is not caused by external events, products, or accumulations of wealth. Happiness is internal and deeply rooted to your choice to be happy, no matter what events you are involved. *Happiness is not based on happenings but on the choices and decisions you make, activities and events you engage that gives meaning, hope, and purpose in your life.*

Happiness can only happen the moment you decide and tell yourself that you will be happy. "I choose to be happy." You are personally responsible for your happiness. Happiness is a choice. Happiness is a decision, not an event. Happiness is 90 percent internal and only 10 percent external. A good illustration is an iceberg: 90 percent of an iceberg is hidden below the sea water and only 10 percent is exposed or made visible. This means external events or activities only contribute 10 percent or less to your happiness. This is in recognition that your environment affects the condition of your feelings. This means you decide your happiness. Meaning, you're in control of your happiness, not your environment. You are the captain of your emotional response with your environment. Environment does not control your happiness. The four seasons or climate change does not dictate the level of your happiness. Outside forces are subjective to your happiness. Happiness is internal happenings more than external events.

*Real happiness is an internal state of the heart.* Real happiness is a result of a series of choices and decisions that you make fulfilling your purpose in life. Real happiness does not come from riches or accumulations of money but finding the real meaning of your life. In other words, happiness is deeply rooted to the meaning of your life, essential to your being. *You are designed by God as a spiritual being to find complete happiness in Him alone!* You are not designed to find happiness on material things or events under the sun. No spiritual being will be completely happy by possessing material things. As a spiritual being, your happiness comes from discovering the meaning of your life, the purpose of your life, and those things that you are hopeful to do.

❧❧❧

## "You are designed by God as a spiritual being to find complete happiness in Him alone!"

**Francis Herras**

❧❧❧

You are designed by God, who is spirit, as a spiritual being to find complete happiness in Him! Events or activities are temporal happiness. Wealth and riches are temporal material things. Lasting happiness and completeness come from God. He alone can complete, fulfill, and satisfy the deepest longing and needs in your heart because He is the one who made you. No one knew you intimately more than God. He knew your need of happiness. The good news is He can make you happy when you allow Him.

Here is a philosophy: I am engaged in fun activities and social events because I am happy not to find happiness elsewhere. Happiness is not out there. Happiness is inside of me. I play golf because I am happy. I play bowling because I am happy. I eat out and socialize with other people because I am happy. I dress up and go to work because I am happy. These engagements are results of happiness from inside of me. Golfing, bowling, fishing, eating out, socializing is not the source of my happiness. I do them because I am happy. I do them because I choose to engage in activities that give meaning and purpose in my life.

Let's take salvation for example. Good works is not good enough to save you from your sins. If your good works is enough to justify you from your sin, no need for Jesus to die and shed His blood on the cross. The only good work that will satisfy to meet the payment and justification of your sins is the good work of Christ—his suffering, crucifixion, death, resurrection, and glorification. In the same manner, you do not engage in fun events or activities to be happy or to find happiness. You do fun activities and social events because you are happy. In other words, you do not do good works to get saved; you do good works because you knew you are saved. You do good works that comes from faith in Christ.

Happiness is not an event; it's a choice you make yourself. You engage on fun things because you are a happy person from the inside first. You knew from your heart; you have the very source of real lasting happiness, not based on external things or events, but on the Person of Jesus Christ who made you. You are happy because you knew you are complete in Christ your Savior, Healer, Sanctifier, and coming King. As a result, your happiness overflows through meaningful activities, which touches and affects others positively.

You do happy stuff because you allow happiness to express itself in a creative and meaningful ways, such as making a difference in the lives of others. You've discovered ways to unleash the happiness inside of you to influence others positively. You allow happiness to exude positive expression of new thoughts and ideas that can transform lives, families, communities, cities and nations of the world that desperately needs to see and understand the real meaning of what happiness is all about. This happiness inside of you is deeply rooted in Christ, roaring like a lion that cannot be contained in the cage of your heart. It roars inside of you. You can feel it. It screams inside like a voice of a thunder unleashed. This happiness inside of you finds creative ways to express itself in ethical ways. This happiness inside of you is deeply rooted in the new life you have in Christ. You are a new creation in Christ. The new life in Christ that is in you is overflowing with happiness. The new life in Christ bubbles up into exceeding happiness. It is the new life in Christ that is the source of real and lasting happiness. Happiness is life being express to please Jesus and point others to Him.

Happiness is life express into the fullest, expressed into its highest potentials, highest meaning, highest purpose, and highest hopes. Happiness is allowing the new life in Christ to manifest its very purpose to seek, save, and serve the lost souls.

Happiness is noticeable and contagious. Happiness cannot be contained; it will express in itself. Happiness is real and felt. When you have it, you know you have it. When you do not have it, it shows in your daily life.

You don't look for happiness—you create happiness by making wise and healthy choices and decisions that brings meaning and purpose in your life. Part of this decision is to make Jesus the center of your life. Put the Prince of Peace at the core of your being. Choose Jesus Christ to be the center of your life. This is the foundation of true, real, and lasting happiness, which can never be stolen from you.

჻

## "You don't look for happiness—you create happiness by making wise and healthy choices and decisions that brings meaning and purpose in your life."

**Francis Herras**

჻

In daily practical application, this mean you are responsible for your happiness. You create your own happiness by creating your daily life's activities in relation with your God-given purpose in life. You create happiness by creating activities that you love to engage. You create happiness by doing things that makes you a better person. Yes, you can create happiness because you have been gifted with life to create it. There is no limit to what you can do to create happy things as a form of expressing your happiness. I'm sure when God was creating the universe it flows from His pure joy and love. He was happy with everything He did in the universe. God Himself said, "It was good." One must remember that God created the universe because He is sovereignly happy. He is the source of happiness. He expresses this happiness through His creation. God creates because He is happy not to find happiness. In the same manner, you create, you work, and you serve because you are happy, not because you want to find happiness. In other words, everything you do is an expression of your happiness and personality.

I must see myself a happy person. I must believe I am a happy person because I have the Source in me. I must develop a deeper level of awareness of the Source in me and realized that my happiness comes from within not from external things. I have every reason to be happy every day because I have the Source within me. I must allow the Source of happiness to express happiness through me to effect and influence others. The Source makes me happy! This happiness expresses to creativity in terms of daily activities in life, meaning, purpose, and hope in life.

*I am made for God's pleasure.* I am God's masterpiece. I am God's highest form of happiness in Christ. I am the crown of God's creation! I was made in happiness and for happiness. I am destined to live happy! I am destined to a happy place called heaven! I am made by God and made for God. I am God's pleasure! I must live this way every day.

Geographical location has nothing to do with happiness. Anywhere I go, I have the Source within me. Location is subjective. The Source is the object of my happiness. I can live a happy life anywhere in the world because I have the Son of God in me who have given me a purpose to live a meaningful life.

## C. The Key to Meaningfulness

The secret to meaningfulness is *embracing God's purpose in your life* and aligning your perspective of life according to God's view.

*"The words of the Teacher, son of David, king in Jerusalem: "Meaningless! Meaningless!" says the Teacher. "Utterly meaningless! Everything is meaningless"* (Ecclesiastes 1:1-2 NIV).

.•.•.•.

## "The secret to meaningfulness is *embracing God's purpose in your life* and aligning your perspective of life according to God's view."

### Francis Herras

.•.•.•.

The Hebrew thought surrounding the word meaningless or vanity here refers concretely to vapor or mist or breath. I believe metaphorically used by the writer to mean something "elusive, hallow, or fleeting."

During winter, the City of Chestermere Lake, where I lived, just fifteen minutes east of Calgary, Alberta, at times is foggy especially at night. Many times upon driving home, 17 Avenue is covered with a thick fog. I literally couldn't see the road and vehicles in front of me. From afar, it looks the fog is solid, but the moment I was in it or under it, it was hollow and elusive. Can't get hold of it, it gets hold of you once you're in it. Anywhere I look I see is fog and a feeling of uncertainty; I get nervous as what could potentially happen even though I have driven that same highway day in and day out. The fog changes everything. It affects my feelings, my thoughts, and my visibility. It affects my approach to be extra careful. It affects my speed and my focus when I look for a point of reference. It gives me that feeling of being lost, yet I'm not because I've driven the same road many times.

The fog totally changed my perspective driving on that same road. It gives me a narrow and limited perspective framed by the thick fog. *The view under the fog is a view without a point of reference.* The thick fog has taken my point of reference to driving. Suddenly, I am no longer enjoying my driving. Yes, I'm still moving forward cautiously slow. The normal ten-minute drive has become a thirty-minute drive sometimes even more.

❧❧❧

## "The view under the fog is a view without a point of reference."

**Francis Herras**

❧❧❧

The fog has gotten me. It gives me a view of what it looks under it and in it. It blinded me from my points of reference to drive normally. The following day, the sun rises, and the fog was gone. It vaporized. The thick concrete-looking fog disappears.

What was in Solomon's mind when he said, *"Vanity of vanities" (Ecclesiastes 1:1-1 NKJV)?* What was he trying to tell himself and us today when he said those words? Was he reminding himself and us today of the truths he discovered on himself, the material things he possessed, the lesson he learned what riches, wealth, possessions, accomplishments, and success can do to you when viewed without God? Was he conveying to himself and us today the lesson he learned the elusiveness and fleeting nature of material things—fame and glory—and the hallow nature of things here on earth? Was he saying that material things and the things of the earth can only give you momentary happiness and satisfaction yet void with meaning?

Literally, Solomon was saying, "I've got everything. You name it, I have it. But here is my issue: I did not find meaning in those things I've got. I did not find the meaning of life in spite of everything—wisdom, riches, wealth, possessions, influence, and success. I still don't understand why I felt life is meaningless as a matter of my personal assessment was "everything is meaningless!" The truth is the very things that I thought important to me are not the very things that matter most in life. Like mist and vapor, those things that I believe and hold on in life will one day disappear. In a blink of an eye, they will vanish like a mist.

The fog in my story, although there's nothing wrong with money, wealth, and possession, they can alter your point of reference in life. *Things and success can suddenly change your view of life. Things have the power to create an elusive, hollow perspective framed by success. Or a perspective, a lens that sees life surrounded with things and defined by things.* The truth is, things can't define your life. Once you've got everything, you could want in life, the tendency is you start creating your own meaning and definition of life. You now see life according to the lens that riches and success handed over to you. You now develop an elusive view of life, a perspective drawn from your riches, a perspective of seeing life and things without any reference to God, the Giver of everything. Solomon was conveying lesson he learned to safeguard us from doing or repeating the same mistake he did. We can learn from Solomon that riches, wealth and success have the power to alter your belief in God to belief in self. It has the power to create and hand you over a perspective without any reference to God or a view of life purely under the sun; to see life without God, the Creator and the very meaning of life.

.ℓ.ℓ.ℓ.

## "Things and success can suddenly change your view of life. Things have the power to create an elusive, hollow perspective framed by success. Or a perspective, a lens that sees life surrounded with things and defined by things."

**Francis Herras**

.ℓ.ℓ.ℓ.

The love of money is in itself is a perspective and belief created by money. In this case, money has made you become the person money intended you to become. It is a form of a belief that says, "I love money more than God." Money in itself is not evil. Money is neutral. Money doesn't have feelings and can't make a decision for you. It is a medium of exchange. We pay the bills with our hard-earned money. Money is important—as a matter of fact, a very important commodity in our daily living. Is money the most important thing in life? Solomon's answer to this question is no. Money is not the most important thing in life. "I have it everything." Meaning is the most important thing in life. *Solomon got money in search for the meaning. Many of us today got meaning in search for money.* May be for others, in the search for both money and meaning! Money is not the problem. The issue is money more than God. The bigger issue is seeing life under the sun purely secular or atheistic frame of reference. I call this view under the fog.

☙☙☙

## "Solomon got money in search for meaning. Many of us today got meaning in search for money."

### Francis Herras

☙☙☙

*The question now is, what has you become?* What did those earthly things, accomplishments, and success made you? Did it make your life more meaningful or meaningless? Was King Solomon conveying to us the fleeting limitation of earthly perspective under the sun? A perspective framed under the sun, a secular view of life. Was he trying to say to himself and us today that putting your hopes on material things is holding into a thick mist or vapor that soon will dissipates? Was Solomon conveying a message to himself and us today that in his search for meaning, the only way to find is to "look above the sun," meaning to look to God who created the universe and who sent His Son, Jesus, who made us a new creation by the virtue of His death and resurrection.

**UPWARD MOMENTUM ACTION STEPS**

*Write your answers on a clean sheet of paper.*

What is your personal *"one thing"*? Elaborate why?

What is the most powerful antidote for loneliness? Explain why?

Describe the key to happiness and why?

What is happiness?

What is meaning? And what is the secret of meaningfulness? How do you intend to apply this in your walk with God?

Explain "view under the fog" in terms of perspective.

# CHAPTER 4

# Humility Embrace the Mindset that Sees the Workings and Hears the Voice of God

*"A lowly person is a teachable person, easily entreated and open to explanation. Many of our spirits are too arrogant: they can teach others but can never themselves be taught. Many possess a stubborn spirit: they stick to their opinions even if they realize they are wrong."*
*- Watchman Nee*

Psalm 29 shows a heart that sees the active workings of God, meditates upon God, and hear Him speak through nature. *Psalm 29, tells me of a mindset that intentionally focuses on the glory of God through the activities of nature.* It unfolds a heart sensitive to "the voice of God" through the phenomenon of nature as described in the chapter in the following verses on capital letters:

> "The *voice of the Lord* is over the WATERS ..." (Psalm 29:3a NIV, emphasis mine)

> "The *God of glory* THUNDERS, the Lord over mighty WATERS." (Psalm 29:3b NIV, emphasis mine)

"The *voice of the Lord* breaks the CEDARS; the Lord breaks in the cedars of *Lebanon.*" (Psalm 29:5 NIV, emphasis mine)

"The *voice of the Lord* strikes with *flashes* of LIGHTNING." (Psalm 29:7 NIV, emphasis mine)

"The *voice of the Lord shakes* the DESERT; the Lord *shakes the DESERT of Kadesh.*" (Psalm 29:8 NIV, emphasis mine)

"The voice of the Yahweh causes DEER give birth *[right in the midst of nature's phenomena]* and strips the FORESTS bare. And at his temple all in it say "GLORY!"" (Psalm 29:9 LEB, insertion and emphasis mine)

"Yahweh sits enthroned at the FLOOD …" (Psalm 29:10 LEB, emphasis mine)

The language used by the writer is very descriptive possibly the author himself is right in the middle of the phenomena watching and reflecting on God's role as the nature's phenomena unfold its expression, power, impact and outcomes. At the end of the day, the writer sees God's Glory behind the phenomenon. When everything is said and done, he hears the voice of the Lord not the disaster, the flood, shaking, breakings, but the voice and the glory of the Lord through nature speaking to get his attention for sure the 21st century civilized people through nature's recent activities who interprets them as "act of mother nature." *There is no such thing as an "act of mother nature," only an act of God speaking through nature's phenomenon to get humanity's attention to listen to what he is saying.* Or to discern what he is saying to me. Is God calling me to turn to him and turn away from sins and evil practice?

๑๑๑

# "There is no such thing as an "act of mother nature," only an act of God speaking through nature's phenomenon to get humanity's attention to listen to what he is saying."

**Francis Herras**

๑๑๑

What is it God telling me through my personal experience through nature as it unfolds before me, the hurricane, tsunami, flooding and earthquake happening often around the globe? Is God calling me and the rest of humanity to humble them and turn away from their sins? Folks, these are not "act of mother nature" but an act of the Sovereign Powerful God of the universe talking to his children made in his image. The only way to find out what God is saying look into His written Word the Bible! It is sad to say that people today believe more on social media or TV news more than God's infallible words in the Bible.

## A. Life Should Measure Time Not Time Measuring Life

Have you ever asked yourself these questions? What is time? What is it? Why do we have it? Where did time originated? What is the purpose of time and space, anyhow? Do we need time and space to live our lives? Did God created time and space just to place his creation to exist in it including human being?

God is not bound by time and space. Time and space can't contain Him. God created both time and space way before the creation of the visible universe. *God is a self-existing God. His nature does not need time nor space.* Time and space cannot measure God. He is totally dependent to nothing but Himself. He is self-existing, powerful and self-sustaining God independent from time and space. Time and space is in his hand. He made them both. *He designs time and space to carry out his purpose.* But, one must realize that God doesn't need time and space to self-exist. Human being does. Furthermore, creation needs space to exist and time to progress. For this purpose, I believe, time and space is essential for God's creation to progress, develop, and evolved within his define space and time.

**.·.·.·.**

## "God is a self-existing God. His nature does not need time nor space. He designs time and space to carry out his purpose."

### Francis Herras

**.·.·.·.**

Did God created the year, seasons, and days so we can measure everything against it as people does today in the different part of society. People use time to measure progress and results. Companies measure applicant employees through their earlier years of employment performance. Everything is measured by time? Your income per hour is measured by your experienced and education. Your mortgage approval is measured by how much you earn per annum (within 365 days). Your work performance is measured within the bounce of your working hours.

Society structured everything according to time. As a matter of fact, we time everything we do so we can measure productivity. We define what time we go to work and end work every day. We set what time we want to eat breakfast, take a shower, go to work, things to do at work and we define how many hours we should have spent in a project. Investment growth is measured by time. Education is measured by time (four years degree). House mortgage is measured by time (25 years). Human life span is measured by time. Essentially everything is measured by time!

## B. Do we really have to Measure Everything by Time?

Many times I wonder do we have to measure everything by time. There's so much emphasis given to time, and the results attributed with it to the point that we're no longer living a life with quality and freedom.

*Everything we do is subjected to time as a result we want more time to do things and to do more at the expense of life.* We have created a strategy that choked swallowed life instead of allowing life to flourished progress and develop naturally without any pressure or being measured up by time.

ℓℓℓ

# "Everything we do is subjected to time as a result we want more time to do things and to do more at the expense of life."

**Francis Herras**

ℓℓℓ

Should not life use time for its favor not the other way around? Shouldn't time be working for the good of life to carry out its ultimate purpose and original design? *Shouldn't life measure time not time measuring life! Shouldn't the barometer of measurement life not time, the quality of life instead of the quality of time.* Shouldn't life the emphasis of existence, not time? Shouldn't life create time, not time creating life? Shouldn't life measure time?

Time must be subjected to life. Life must run time not time running life. Time must serve life and should be working for life not the other way. *Time must be utilized to achieve life's highest purpose. Time is a tool to carry out your purpose not life.*

Life must manage time not time managing life. Life is a living organism, time is not. Time is neutral and lifeless. Life is a precious gift from God as well as time, but the highest form of gift is life. Life is so precious that Jesus poured out his own blood to redeem life made in God's image and likeness not time. Time is a tool, an instrument to do everything we wanted to do in life. *Life has never been designed to be a tool or instrument of time or anybody. So, time should serve life's purpose not life serving time.*

# "Life has never been designed to be a tool or instrument of time or anybody. So, time should serve life's purpose not life serving time."

### Francis Herras

♪♪♪

I've heard many people say, *"I need more time."* What they are saying is, *"I need more life."* Others say, *"I don't have time."* What they are saying is, *"I don't have life."* Why is this? The answer is simple; time run's their life instead of life running their time. When you find yourself saying, I need more time or I don't have time that is an indicator that you are asking for more life. What you are saying is, "I am not living my life to the fullest as I should." In this case, you exist, use by time without accomplishing your highest potential and purpose.

## C.  What we Really Need is More Life Not More Time

The hard fact is God has provided humanity the time needed from the beginning when he created the universe and when he placed the first couple Adam and Eve in the Garden of Eden - a home, he made for them. God has provided time and space for the first couple to live their life together with God their Creator. Time and space was provided for them to grow in relationships, evolved, progress and develop to their highest potential and ultimate purpose. *The problem is people today allow time and space to use them apart from God.* They have abandon Life in exchange for the time as a result; they have more time without quality of life.

*Space and time was designed not to measure life but as an essential tool to advance life to flourish.* Time and space has been given for humanity to develop according to God's design, not to abuse time, or purely occupy space but to seize time to live life in relationship with God and to give life plenty of space to grow, mature, celebrate, and experience its Creator!

Is it possible to allow life to flourish in its highest potential and purpose in any given condition without measuring it up with time? Is it possible to allow life progress, develop and mature wherever we are—at home, at work, business, school or ministry without so much emphasis on time? *Shouldn't life be the focal point of existence than time; doing more life in time than doing more time in life?* Shouldn't we value more life more than time? *When life is valued and elevated, time becomes secondary because we've discovered life is more valuable than time.* When you are in this position, your life will always be catching for life. Life should be the focus in everything you do. Life should be valued more than time.

ℓℓℓ

**"Shouldn't life be the focal point of existence than time; doing more life in time than doing more time in life? When life is valued and elevated, time becomes secondary because we've discovered life is more valuable than time."**

**Francis Herras**

ℓℓℓ

**D. Time did not Create Life, Life Creates Time**

"Then the LORD God formed a man from the dust of the ground and **breathed** into his nostrils **the breath of life**, and the man became a living being" (Genesis 2:7 NIV, emphasis mine).

Life originated from the inmost being of God. God "**breathed**" "the breath of life" to man. This means you have the "breath" of God in you "the breath of life" that makes you human—a living being. **It is the "breath" of God that made you alive not time.** You came from the inmost being of your Maker not solely to consume time but to live your life to the fullest.

*Life creates time! Life design time!* Life use time not the other way! It is in this discovery that we realize that *the focus of life is living out its potentials,*

47

*gifts, talents, skills and highest purpose that it was designed.* Life should live, grow, develop, progress, and flourish according to its design. ***Time should serve life and the purpose of life!*** Time is an essential space for life to do its purpose, that is, live in relationship with its Creator. *What humanity needs today is not more time but more life! Yes, more life with their Creator, their loved ones and God's family!*

♪♪♪

## "What humanity needs today is not more time but more life! Yes, more life with their Creator, their loved ones and God's family!"

**Francis Herras**

♪♪♪

## E. What Humanity Needs Today is More Life

Life and time are gifts from God not only to enjoy but likewise to live life to its purpose and design.

What you need today is more life! Life with God! Life with your spouse and children! Life with God's people (the church) living life together, experiencing life together, celebrating life together, growing life together, enjoying life together, and living out life's purpose together in relationship with Jesus Christ our Lord and Savior. *What you need today is a quality of life living out your purpose more than a quality of time.*

To enjoy your life your must understand its purpose. Pay attention to the Giver of life. Live your life connected with God! *I think the secret of life is life live with God and his children.* ***Your life with God—life to Life together in time!*** More of God more of life! More of Jesus more of his life! More of God's Word more of his knowledge, wisdom, and power to live life. Today, what we need is more life more than time. Quality of life in relationship with Jesus, loved ones and neighbors.

.ı.ı.ı.

# "What you need today is a quality of life living out your purpose more than a quality of time."

**Francis Herras**

.ı.ı.ı.

---

**UPWARD MOMENTION ACTION STEPS**

*Write your answers on a clean sheet of paper.*

How would you define time in your own words
in your current context of life?

Is there a correlation between life, time and space?

Do you find yourself saying "I need more time?" and why?

What is your perspective of life?

---

# CHAPTER 5

# Humility is Being Still to Know God

*"Our failure to hear His voice when we want to is due to the fact that we do not in general want to hear it, that we want it only when we think we need it."[51]*
— *Dallas Willard*

"Be **STILL**, and **KNOW** that <u>I am God</u>. I will be exalted among the <u>nations</u>; I will be exalted in the <u>earth</u>!" (Psalm 46:10 KJV, emphasis mine)

We lived in a noisy world with manufactured noises that invades the tranquility God wants us to experience. Our minds is bombarded with voices from the television; newspapers and magazines; the voices of the people around us home, work, ministry and business; the raging noise of vehicles; the social media noises; and voice of the enemy. These voices bombard your mind consumed your time and energy to the point of depletion and fatigue due to noise overload. Over and above this overload, fear, worries, doubts, and a feeling of uncertainty, confusion is increasing.

Is there a way out of these? Absolutely! The Word of God tells us in Psalm "Be **STILL** and **KNOW** that <u>I am God</u>. I will be exalted among the <u>nations</u>; I will be exalted in the <u>earth</u>!" (Psalm 46:10 KJV, emphasis mine)

---

[51] Willard, Dallas. "Hearing God: Developing a Conversational Relationship with God." 2017. https://www.goodreads.com/work/quotes/400663-hearing-god-developing-a-conversational-relationship-with-god. November 23, 2017.

**"Be still"** and discover God's will for your life. God cares for you so much that He wants you to "be still." This necessitates you **decide** to examine, analyze and assess the quality, priorities and condition of your life; stop, look and listen to what is happening in your life at this moment; take a deep breath to examine the state of your heart, this idea is the greatest gift you can ever reward yourself to "be still."

A good illustration is your vehicle. After driving at least 10,000 kilometers it needs change oil and sometimes requires flushing out used corroded oil to keep your vehicle in good condition, up and running so you can drive safe with peace of mind. When you ignore to change oil to flush out dirty oil from your vehicle the engine will breakdown. This mindset may cause havoc in your life, your loved ones and other people. Your vehicle is designed to handle clean oil. You must pay attention to the condition and state of your vehicle and do the maintenance recommended by the manufacturer for your own safety and vehicle functionality.

To *"be still"* is taking time to read the warning signs in the dashboard of your heart, find areas of your life that needs your immediate attention. Meaning slow or stop to flush out whatever is stressing you out to clean the junks from your heart, a time to repentance for spiritual, emotional and mental refreshment. This posture flush out the voices and noises of the world from your mind so you can fill it up with fresh oil of the Holy Spirit; thoughts and ideas coming from God's Word; fresh knowledge of God and a brand new perspective related to your life's purpose.

**"Be STILL …"**

It is hard to change oil and flush oil from a moving vehicle in the same manner hard to refresh a busy and overloaded heart and mind. *"Be still"* and then *"know"* for in the stillness that knowing deepens. *A life changing ideas arises from stillness in God's presence makes purpose and dreams become clearer than ever.*

.ℓ.ℓ.ℓ

## "A life changing ideas arises from stillness in God's presence makes purpose and dreams become clearer than ever."

### Francis Herras

.ℓ.ℓ.ℓ

Stillness precedes knowing. Knowing comes when the heart and mind is ready and prepared. *It is in the stillness of heart that great ideas, dreams and visions are conceived.* In stillness the voices of the world are flushed out put you in a strategic place to hear God's still small voice louder than any voices. It is in the stillness you positioned yourself to learn new things, know God until the noises of this fallen world ceased from your heart and mind; the things of this world becomes smaller God becomes bigger in your life; Jesus Christ at the throne of your heart; his voice becomes clearer louder every day of your life; your faith arises from hearing and hearing the Word of God the voice of God; until you become the person God wants you to be!

.ℓ.ℓ.ℓ

## "It is in the stillness of heart that great ideas, dreams and visions are conceived."

### Francis Herras

.ℓ.ℓ.ℓ

### "...KNOW I am GOD"

Is there greater knowledge than the knowledge of God? Is there greater learning than knowing your Creator who made and designed you for a greater purpose? *True learning ceases when God is set aside and not in the equation information*; knowing who God is the highest form of knowledge that one can ever have in his entire life on this planet.

Listen to God's invitation, *"Be STILL, and KNOW I am GOD."* In his own words, he says, *"I am God!"* I am Supreme, Sovereign, Ultimate Power, Cause of the universe, God who made you.

If God is what He said He is, then the glory belongs to Him alone! The *self* is abased, the *world* is abased, the *voices* and *noises* dethroned so Christ is enthroned in your heart; the *glory* and *glitters* of the world subsides only the glory and majesty of Jesus shines in your life in an ever increasing manner.

May God fill your mind with His knowledge, may his glory refresh your spirit, soul and body. Experience his peace, joy, wisdom, love and abundance until you overflow with his presence.

---

**UPWARD MOMENTION ACTION STEPS**

*Write your answers on a clean sheet of paper.*

What comes to your mind when you hear God's Word, "Be **STILL** and **KNOW** that I am God …? Psalm 46:3 elaborate how you can apply this in your life.

Are there warning signs in the dashboard of your heart that needs your immediate attention?

How do you describe the state of your mind and spirit? Why?

Are you growing in the knowledge of God's Word? When was the last time you read your Bible? Why?

---

# CHAPTER 6

# Humility Serves and Follow Jesus to Win in Life

*"Let God have your life; He can do more with it than you can."*[52]
*- Dwight L. Moody*

*"Whoever loves his life loses it, and whoever hates his life in this world will keep it for eternal life. If anyone <u>serves me</u>, he must <u>follow me</u>; and where I am, there will <u>my servant</u> be also. If anyone <u>serves me</u>, the <u>Father will honor him</u>."(John 12:25-26 NIV)*

## A.  The Problem in the Journey of Life

We've been captivated by *"things"* and *"stuff"* in our earthly journey. We're distracted by wonderful and interesting things—life itself, our family, our ministry, our work, our business and social activities. Suddenly, we're enjoying the *"things,"* the *"stuff,"* the *"events,"* the *"activities,"* the *"business,"* the *"family and life"* more than God.

God was removed from the journey subtly; then we began to develop a perspective within the *"framework of things, stuff, family and life"* away from God. We now start defining things according to things and stuff. We start defining our lives according to what we have and start looking

---

[52] Moody, Dwight L. "18 Beautiful Christian Quotes Humility." https://www.christianquotes.info/top-quotes/18-beautiful-christian-quotes-about-humility/#axzz4n6Het3cv. November 23, 2017.

life according to "things and stuff" more than looking it according to the framework of God the author of life. Like King Solomon, we now see and define life *"under the sun."* Our belief and perspective was altered by the earthly "things and stuff."

**The point is the *fanfare* of the journey has gotten into our hearts and minds!** *We've become a "fun and happy" conscious people than God's purpose conscious people.* The journey itself has become more enjoyable than the companionship of God who gave us life and purpose. We now start pursuing life and our dreams apart from God.

We start measuring things according to our own standards more than God's moral standard. We start telling ourselves it's okay, just do it. God will understand. We start thinking we're okay, safe and secured when we abandon our safety and security in life God Himself. The One who is able to do exceedingly abundantly more than we could ever ask or imagine! We abandon the very Source of life itself.

We've abandon the only Jesus who can give us real lasting joy and peace in the midst of turbulent times where we are now in history. We've abandon the very Reason of our existence and purpose of our existence. We've abandon the only One that loves us unconditionally and the very definition and meaning of our existence. We've abandoned the God who completes us; satisfies us and fill us with his Holy Spirit to live a life pleasing to Him. By going ahead of God in the journey of life, we've basically abandoned everything that is good for us and the only One that cares and knew our destiny.

**We've become worshippers of *"things and stuff"* than worshippers of God.** We've become motivated by things and stuff than motivated by God's purpose. We've become a people driven by culture, money, success, fame, position and great accomplishments more than enjoying God and knowing God intimately in the life's journey.

***In the journey of life our highest goal is not our top 10 goals but God!*** Loving God with our heart, soul, strength and mind should be our highest goal in life. Loving and knowing God more is supposed to be life's highest goal. *"Love the Lord your God with all your heart and with all your soul and with all your strength and with all your mind." (Matthew 6:33 NIV)*

❦❦❦

## "In the journey of life our highest goal is not our top 10 goals but God! Loving God with our heart, soul, strength and mind should be our highest goal in life."

**Francis Herras**

❦❦❦

Experiencing God, his love, peace, joy, holiness, words, promises, plans and purpose for our lives should be our highest goals in life the spirit of true humility. Experiencing his provisions and protection and his Being should be our highest priority and then *"all these things"* we needed shall be added unto us our Lord Jesus said it. *"But seek first his kingdom and his righteousness, and all these things will be given to you as well."* (Matthew 6:33 NIV)

Jesus knew God's ultimate purpose and design for our lives. He knew what it will take to carry out your purpose. Jesus knew the necessary resources to carry out your ultimate design in life till you reach your final destiny. God has the resources you need to move you forward. His resources are more than enough when you seek Him and put Him first. *God first means God at the top of everything in your life. This is the order of life.* When God is at the core of your being the motivation of everything in your life, things are in order, the resources you needed are provided.

❦❦❦

## God first means God at the top of everything in your life. This is the order of life.

**Francis Herras**

❦❦❦

**So, enjoy God more than the journey.** Enjoy God more than life itself. Experience God more than life, family and business; let God be at the core of your life, family, work and ministry and these things that you worry will be added unto you.

*"If anyone serves me, he must follow me"* *(John 12:26 ESV)*

Anyone who chooses to *serve* Jesus must *follow* Jesus. Anyone who chooses to love Jesus and decided to serve Jesus must choose to *follow Jesus' teachings* and kingdom principles. Serving and following goes hand in hand when one chose to serve Jesus' purpose.

"*If* anyone *serves* me, he must *follow* me …" Serving Jesus is a product of your choice. Following Jesus is a product of your will. God has given you the capacity and ability to make choices and decisions as a rational being. God will never force anyone to serve him and follow him. He may call someone to do a specific ministry or kingdom work on earth through the prompting of the Holy Spirit but totally up to that person to respond to God's call and say, "Yes I'll do it because I chose to and willingly give my life to Jesus for eternal purposes."

*"If anyone serves me, the Father will honor him."* *(John 12:26 ESV, emphasis mine)*

Serving and following Jesus will always be rewarded. God is a God of reward. He is a very generous God. You cannot out give God! When you give your life to serve Jesus and follow Jesus the Father will *honor* you. Your service and commitment to Jesus is acknowledged and recognized by the Father nothing that you do for Jesus and his kingdom escape from his eyes. Jesus promised you will be honored by the Father—the highest honor one can get!

*"…the Father will honor him."* *(John 12:26 ESV)*

Who knows what encapsulates within that honor. But I do believe the Fathers' honor is a good thing, satisfying and lasting honor. To be honored by God the Creator of the universe is the highest form of reward one can ever have in this life on earth and the life to come in eternity. Everything you do for Jesus will be rewarded! *Every good works done in faith will be rewarded commensurately.* This is your upward momentum!

✎✎✎

# "Every good works done in faith will be rewarded commensurately."

## Francis Herras

✎✎✎

The good thing being honored by God is that God has to choose what he desires to reward you. You don't have to worry the reward because God has the best for you. God sees your deepest needs and desires in life. He is aware of your family needs, marital needs, financial needs, emotional needs, psychological needs, physiological needs, social needs, business needs and most of your spiritual needs. Who knows what God will give you in terms of his promised honor and rewards to those who choose to serve and follow Jesus?

✎✎✎

# "Serving and following Jesus is choosing to win in life and the life to come."

## Francis Herras

✎✎✎

*Serving and following Jesus is choosing to win in life and the life to come.* Choosing Jesus is choosing to win. This is your upward momentum! When you chose Jesus, you choose to honor the Father. When you are honored by the Father the glitters of this world doesn't matter anymore. Absolutely no appeal to you because you've found the real Treasure of heaven, the bright morning Star, the Lily of the Valley, Balm of Gilead, the King of kings and the Lord of lords. This is your upward momentum that will propel you to your forward momentum!

*When you chose to serve Jesus, you choose to win.* When you chose to follow Jesus you choose to win. When you chose Jesus more than the things of this world, you choose the honor of the heavenly Father. The good thing your choices is that you will live what He designed your life to be; the Father will empower you to live according to his original intent and purpose for your life. You have nothing to lose when you choose Jesus except your sins and Christless eternity. You have the reason to become the person God designed you be in Christ. You have the reason to be successful in Christ. In Christ you are always a winner! You are more than conqueror. In Christ you are saved, sanctified, satisfied and complete.

*When you chose to serve Jesus, you choose to win!*

ﭢﭢﭢ

# "When you chose to serve Jesus, you choose to win!"

## Francis Herras

ﭢﭢﭢ

Life is a choice but the greatest choice that you can ever make today is to choose Christ to reign at the core of your being!

---

**UPWARD MOMENTION ACTION STEPS**

*Write your answers on a clean sheet of paper.*

How would you explain "In the journey of our life our highest goal is not our top 10 goals but God."

How would respond to Jesus' words, "If anyone serves me, he must follow me …" (John 12:16 ESV)

Are you serving and following Jesus? Why?

---

# CHAPTER 7

# Humility Balances Practice and Posture

*"Humble souls are fearful of their own strength."*
*- William Gurnall*

"Offer to God a *sacrifice of thanksgiving*, and *perform your vows* to the Most High, and *call upon me in the day of trouble*; I will deliver you and you shall glorify me." (Psalm 50:14-15 ESV, emphasis mine)

Here is an excellent picture of contrast between *practice and posture*. God was speaking to his people as the holy judge of the universe— "Hear, O my people, and I will speak; O Israel, I will testify AGAINS YOU. *I am God your God*. Not for your sacrifice do I rebuke you; your burnt offerings are continually before me. I will not accept a bull from your house or goats from your folds. For every beast of the forest is mine, the cattle on a thousand hills. I know all the birds of the hills, and all that moves in the field is mine. If I were hungry, I would not tell you, for the world and its fullness are mine. Do I eat the flesh of bulls or drink the blood of goats." (Psalm 50:7-13 ESV). According to God's assessment, *"Not for your SACRIFICE do I rebuke you; your burnt offerings are continually before me." (Psalm 50:8 ESV, emphasis mine)*. The Israelites continually do their burnt offerings as their sense of duty to worship God. God was not against their practice of burnt offerings. He did not tell them to stop their burnt offering to Him, but he told them, *"I will not accept"* (v.9) your rituals or your practice. I have something against you. You are doing it unacceptable. You are missing the mark. *You have the practice without the posture of heart. You have forgotten that your offerings are in itself a representation of the state of your heart.* My issue for you is your heart is dissociated from your burnt offerings. I see your practice and smell the aroma of your offerings but I don't see and smell the aroma of your heart with your burnt offerings. Your burnt offerings and your heart are disconnected. Your offerings ascend without your heart thus become unacceptable before me.

ꞏꞏꞏ

## "You have the practice without the posture of heart. God is against insincere and heartless practice. The posture of your heart does matter to God."

### Francis Herras

ꞏꞏꞏ

God's argument was valid. "For every beast of the forest is mine, the cattle on a thousand hills. I know all the birds of the hills, and all that moves in the field is mine. If I were hungry, I would not tell you, for the world and its fullness are mine. Do I eat the flesh of bulls or drink the blood of goats." (Psalm 50:10-13 ESV). Every living creature that moves on the planet belongs to God before the Israelites offer burnt offerings. The point of offering them back to God doesn't make sense without the very intent of the burnt offering *the posture of their hearts in worship and thanksgiving.* The Israelites were offering their burnt offering to God without the real substance; heartless burnt offering; practice without a posture; burnt offering that is not acceptable to God. *God is against this practice, insincere and heartless practice*— "Hear, O my people, and I will speak; O Israel, *I will testify AGAINST YOU.* I am God your God." (Psalm 50:7 ESV, emphasis mine). In other words, don't do this to me as your God. It is your heart that I want not your offerings.

God is against heartless offering; heartless prayers; heartless service; heartless giving; heartless worship; heartless work and performance for

Him and His Kingdom. *The posture of your heart does matter before God.* When you are serving and following Christ, the state of your heart is extremely essential in God's eyes. The posture of your heart—your intent, motive and content is what matters to Him most. *In the sight of God, what you are becoming is more valuable than what you are doing. God is more interested in your being than in your doing.* This was the problem with the Israelites; they are doing without becoming the being God wants them to be.

♪♪♪

## "In the sight of God, what you are becoming is more valuable than what you are doing. God is more interested in your being than in your doing."

**Francis Herras**

♪♪♪

*Posture precedes practice. Being precedes doing.* God looks into the heart; He looks into the inner sanctum of your being. He is more interested in the inward activities of your daily living. The question is what has you become? Did you become a better person? Did your service move you closer to Jesus?

Jesus is more interested in what you are becoming as his child in practicing the essentials and fundamentals of faith. *Your service and your heart must together ascend into the throne of God not just your service.* This is the case with the Israelites, for that reason God rejected their burnt offerings. As a loving Father, he rebuked and corrected them for their own good and benefits. God wants his children to do things right to put their heart in what they do especially for God or in matters of daily faith practices.

We can't bribe God with our good deeds and live a disobedient life style. God loves good deeds as a matter-of-fact Christians are made for good works and to do good works. *The problem is not the act of doing good works. The problem is heartless good works a plain performance not done in faith in service to God but for the sake of practice.* Drug lords and thief do good works but lacks lifestyle that pleases God. Good works must be a fruit of intimate relationship with Jesus Christ; good works that is the fruit of righteousness done in faith in Christ for His glory. Otherwise, plain good deeds become a bribe to please God. This is unacceptable to God.

☙☙☙

## "The problem is not the act of doing good works. The problem is heartless good works a plain performance not done in faith in service to God but for the sake of practice."

### Francis Herras

☙☙☙

In this passage of scripture God desires for His children to offer a sacrifice of thanksgiving. "Offer to God a *sacrifice of thanksgiving*, and *perform your vows* to the Most High, and *call upon me in the day of trouble*; I will deliver you and you shall glorify me." (Psalm 50:14 ESV)

What is a sacrifice of thanksgiving? *A sacrifice of thanksgiving is an inner posture of the heart.* Thanksgiving is the language of a humble heart. It is the state of the heart that pleases God. It is the heart that recognizes and acknowledges that He is God the owner of everything in the universe. It is a heart that gives thanks to God in everything no matter what. Thanksgiving is an acknowledgment of God Himself. Thanksgiving to God is the recognition that God is actively involved in one's life. Thanksgiving is telling God that he owns everything including your life because of that truth you are grateful. *A sacrifice of thanksgiving is an inner posture of the heart. Thanksgiving is the language of a humble heart.*

☙☙☙

# "A sacrifice of thanksgiving is an inner posture of the heart. Thanksgiving is the language of a humble heart."

## Francis Herras

☙☙☙

It is hard for proud people to say thank you or thank God because their mindset tells them it's because of them not God. Thanksgiving is a form of appreciation and acceptance of God's active involvement in your life.

Thanksgiving is a humble posture of the heart. Thanksgiving is an expression of total dependent upon God and total trust in what He is doing in your daily life. Thanksgiving redirect your focus to God than yourself. Thanksgiving sets you free from being self-centered to Christ-centered. Thanksgiving is total recognition that God is the owner of everything and you are his steward of creation. This is embracing God's view everyone should know. This is heavenly view in motion a view from the top.

## A. Something Greater

As I thought on what Jesus said in Matthew 12, I begin to see how Jesus shows who he was among the people and how he unfolds the state of the heart of the people.

In verse 6 Jesus proclaims to the people and say, "I tell you, SOMETHING greater than the ***temple*** is here" (Matthew 12:6 ESV). Note Jesus said something not someone. And then "For the Son of Man is the lord of the ***Sabbath.***" (Matthew 12:8 ESV) These was Jesus' response to the accusation of the religious people (Pharisees) on the acts of his disciples in verse one. Thus the Pharisees was accusing and judging not only Jesus' disciples but Jesus himself as well. The accusation was triggered by the action of the disciples. The *"disciples were hungry, and they began to pluck heads of grain and to eat"* (Matthew 12:1 ESV). The religious leaders interpreted the disciples act as "not lawful on the Sabbath" (Matthew

64

12:2 ESV). But, they said this not because they care fulfilling the Sabbath but to find fault on Jesus so they can justify their evil plot to kill him. Jesus response to the accusation was "For the Son of Man is the lord of the **Sabbath**" (Matthew 12:8 ESV, emphasis mine). By this, *Jesus was declaring to the people He is—the Lord of the Sabbath! Here Jesus publicly announced He is the Lord of the Sabbath.* Meaning He is greater than the Sabbath, greater than religious rules. Jesus proclaims he is the fulfillment of the Sabbath itself. In other words, Jesus argued that there was nothing violated; nothing unlawful was done by his disciples because He is the Lord of the Sabbath. Yet in spite of Jesus unfolding revelation of who He is, the people did not get it nor believe him instead plan to kill him. *The Pharisees and the people rejected the Lord of the Sabbath to embrace the Sabbath.* They chose not to believe in Jesus because the state of their heart is evil according to Jesus. Jesus calls them *"evil and adulterous generation"* in verse 39.

Listen to Jesus' proclamation to people closely:

> "I tell you, SOMETHING (not someone) greater than the *temple* is here" (Matthew 12:6 ESV).

> "SOMETHING greater than *Jonah* is here," (Matthew 12:41 ESV)

> "SOMETHING greater than *Solomon* is here," (Matthew 12:42 ESV)

*First Jesus proclaims He is the Lord of the Sabbath and then declares publicly something greater than the temple, Jonah, and Solomon is before their very eyes.* Obviously Jesus was communicating *"something greater is here."* What is this something greater than Sabbath and the temple Jesus was referring? People obviously are not getting what Jesus was alluding. Their minds were so occupied by their own rules, belief and traditions not on the truth Jesus was bringing to their attention. The peoples mind was so close especially the religious leaders that they literally fail to understand a very important message Jesus was telling them - who He is, what He is and what He was showing them. They are not getting it.

I am sure when Jesus said *"something greater is here"* he was referring to THE KINGDOM OF GOD IS HERE ON EARTH through his presence. Yet the people didn't get it in spite of the fact Jesus told them face-to-face that the Kingdom of God has come upon them in His presence; that God's Kingdom is greater than any earthly kingdom, the temple they embraced and greater than the prophets they embraced.

Jesus proclaims to the people THE KINGDOM OF GOD IS HERE before your eyes but you refuse to see, believe and receive it because of your evil heart and traditions. Literally, Jesus announced publicly the KING OF THE KINGDOM IS HERE ON EARTH BEFORE YOUR VERY EYES! Have a look. I'm here. Open your eyes and ears. The King of the kingdom of heaven has come to dwell with you, open your hearts. The signs are over you but you refuse to believe and receive God's kingdom because your hearts are evil.

Jesus came to introduce the Kingdom of God through His presence. Obviously Jesus made a contrast between the Kingdom of God (KOG) and kingdom of earth (KOE) by their fruit. The fruit that Jesus saw among the people was the fruit of the earthly kingdom; Jesus used the analogy of "the tree" to make a point of the state of their heart. *The state of the heart and perspective of the people shows which kingdom is reigning in their heart.* The tree is known by its fruit. The king is known by which kingdom he is. In the same manner the people is known by which king and kingdom they belong because of the principles and the belief they embraced. Obviously, accusing Jesus was not a kingdom of God mindset. Planning to kill Jesus was not a kingdom of God mindset. Evidence the kingdom of God was not present in the hearts of the people as a nation. Jesus came to introduce the Kingdom of God through his presence. What a sad news the King of the kingdom of God was present but rejected by his own people! *"He came to his own, and his own people did not receive him"* (John 12:11 ESV). *Jesus came to introduce the Kingdom of God through his presence.* Those who believe and receive him were given a right to become children of God. *"But to all who did receive him, who believed in his name, he gave the right to become children of God, who were born, not of blood nor of the will of the flesh nor of the will of man, but of God"* (John 1:12-13 ESV).

❧❧❧

# "Jesus came to introduce the Kingdom of God through his presence and his teachings."

## Francis Herras

❧❧❧

Here is a question to ponder. Is the kingdom of God reigning in your heart? Is the King of the kingdom reigning in your life? Jesus is the King of the kingdom of God! Do you believe in what he said who he is? Why not make Jesus the King of your life? Will you open your heart and receive Him as your King, Lord and Savior right now? Will you invite him into your heart right now? If your answer is yes, then let's pray the prayer of acceptance.

> "Lord Jesus, I'm yours. Forgive me for my sins, for not believing you and your words. Come into my heart. I confess with my mouth and believe with my heart that you are the Christ who came to save the lost. I open my heart; accept you as the Lord of my life and my Savior. Amen."

If you prayed that prayer today you become a child of God and part of His big kingdom family of the redeemed. *"If you declare with your mouth, "Jesus is Lord," and believe in your heart that God raised him from the dead, you will be saved. For it is with your heart that you believe and are justified, and it is with your mouth that you profess your faith and are saved."* *(Romans10:9-10 NIV)*

Today you become a child of God His presence dwells in you through His Holy Spirit. Today you are forgiven, cleansed from your sins, set free from eternal condemnation. You are now part of God's family in Christ.

## B. The Earth's Core

According to the National Geographic the core is the hottest, densest part of the Earth. "The churning metal of the outer **core** creates and sustains Earth's magnetic field. The hottest part of the core is the Bullen Discontinuity where temperatures reach 6,000° Celsius (10,800° Fahrenheit)—as hot as the surface of the sun. The inner core is a hot, dense ball of (mostly) iron."[53]

Furthermore, the "Earth's magnetic field is crucial to life on our planet. It protects the planet from the charged particles of the solar wind. Without the shield of the magnetic field, the solar wind will strip Earth's atmosphere of the ozone layer that protects life from harmful ultraviolet radiation."[54]

## C. The Earth's Core Make Sense

Without the core the Earth will be destroyed. The core makes sense. It protects and holds up everything. God in his sovereign wisdom and power designed and structured the Earth to be that way. He put order in it. *The earth's core is His idea.* He makes it work according to his good intent and purpose for everything on the planet. Without the core the earth will be out of control if not devastated and strip off of any life's form.

God's design of Earth's core makes sense. His idea of earth's layers and its elements makes sense. It works so. He controls the earth. This makes *God the Center of the universe He* designed with complete order. God caused the universe into existence with order. He is the life, order and sustainer of the universe He created. In short, God runs His universe.

So let me ask you this question, who is running your life? Who is the center of your life? Is Jesus at the core of your being? I want you to look deep into your heart and see who's at its core.

Is Jesus the center of your life? Remember, without the "earth's core" the planet earth will be out of order and devastated. The earth's core is a very important part of the earth's existence and life preservation.

---

[53] National Geographic. "The core is the hottest, densest part of the Earth." 1996-2017. http://www.nationalgeographic.org/encyclopedia/core/. Sept. 18, 2017.
[54] Ibid

So the question is who's at the core of your being? Without Jesus your life will be out of order and contrary to his will and purpose. Why not make Jesus the center of your being? You can invite Jesus by letting Him in your heart as Lord and Savior of your life. He has the power to bring order in your life and flourish into the person he made you to be. Make Jesus the center of your life, marriage, family, work, business, ministry, finances and relationships today. *Jesus at the core of your being is your greatest upward momentum in life!*

꙳꙳꙳

## "The Earth's core makes sense. Jesus at the core of your being is your greatest upward momentum in life!"

**Francis Herras**

꙳꙳꙳

---

### UPWARD MOMENTION ACTION STEPS

*Write your answers on a clean sheet of paper.*

Will God have an issue with you of heartless worship and insincere practice?

In your own words explain the difference between practice and posture and how will you apply this in your own life?

Describe the essence of your personal worship and service to God?

Is Jesus at the core of your being?

---

# CHAPTER 8

# Humility Embraces the True Light and Sees Life Crucified with Christ

*"The greatest day in your life and mine is when we take total responsibility for our attitudes. That's the day we truly grow up."[55]*
*John C. Maxwell*

*"I have been crucified with Christ. It is no longer I who live, BUT CHRIST WHO LIVES IN ME. And the life I now live in the flesh I live by faith in the Son of God, who love and gave himself for me" (Galatians 2:20 NKJV, emphasis mine).*

The great apostle Paul claims *"but Christ who lives in me."* Paul declares the resurrected Christ is alive at the center of his being. Paul's claim evokes *a trade-in transaction* for his "old life style" for Christ life. This trade-in is the only way for Paul and anyone desires to live a Christian life to overcome the weakness of the "old sinful nature" the root of sinful acts, thoughts and self destruction. The only way for the "old self" or the "sinful self" or the "old life style" to die or be under control is for Christ's life at the core of your being - spirit, soul and body - meaning Christ bringing

---

[55] Maxwell, John C. "18Beautiful Christian Quotes About Humility." 2017. https://www.christianquotes.info/top-quotes/18-beautiful-christian-quotes-about-humility/#axzz4n6Het3cv. November 23, 2017.

order in your life. It need humility and complete surrender for this trade-in to happen.

The only way for the "earthly mindset" or "worldly pattern" lifestyle or "old sinful nature" to be subdued is through the indwelling Christ reigning in the throne of your heart. Without Jesus at the core of your heart it will be impossible for you to live a Christian life pleasing to God.

The apostle Paul claims that his "old self" have been crucified with Jesus and that he is embracing the life of Jesus; allowing the new life in Jesus flourish, grow, shape and transform his inner life; allowing the mind of Christ to manifest; and transform his life into the very likeness of his Master. *Jesus was Paul's upward momentum that radically transformed his entire inner and outer being.* The apostle Paul indeed captures the view from the top.

The new life in Christ can only be *"live by faith in the Son of God"* in humility. The only way for Christ's life to flourish in one's life is to live totally connected, absolutely committed to who Christ is. *A person who claims to know Jesus must live an upward momentum life - a fully surrendered and crucified life every moment.*

෴

## "A person who claims to know Jesus must live an upward momentum life – a fully surrendered and crucified life every moment."

**Francis Herras**

෴

The number one evidence of authentic faith is a total commitment to Jesus, his teachings and everything He did. Faith without works is dead. Real faith manifests an intimate relationship with Jesus and with others. Faith in Christ means loving God with your heart, soul, and mind and with your strength. True faith and good works goes together.

Faith in Christ gives birth to a new lifestyle; godly priorities in life; godly living; and godly mindset, so that when people around you look at you they see the life of Christ, the indwelling Christ in you the hope of glory.

Humility embraces the True Light. *"I am the light of the world. Whoever follows me will not walk in darkness, but will have the light of life" (John 8:12 ESV, emphasis mine).*

Jesus declared boldly *"I am the light of the world."* Here Jesus was not referring to the literal light you see in your home you can turn on and off. The truth is no shortage of this light in many forms, colors and luminosity. This light has been a part of human daily existence at home, at work, at church, at the mall and many other places where light is needed. You see these lights around you. It becomes an essential need to human existence. Thank God for Thomas Edison for not quitting until he discovered the right formula to create light you and I enjoy today. But, in spite of these great inventions that lit up our homes *what people needs today is The True Light of the world—Jesus!*

ℰℰℰ

# "What people needs today is The True Light of the world - Jesus!"

## Francis Herras

ℰℰℰ

You may literally have the unique, expensive and sophisticated chandelier in your home but still in darkness. Your home and office may as bright as the sun but still in darkness. You may love the warm light of the sun, moon, and stars but still in darkness.

You can have the lights available on the planet but still live in darkness? Here is why? These lights are *external lights* they don't have the power to penetrate into your spirit and soul. The sunlight may heal your skin or wounds but it can't heal your inner being. The heat of the light may warm the baby inside an incubator but it will not lighten up the baby's inner soul. The baby may warm, comforted and cared for but does not necessarily lighten up his or her inmost being.

In the same manner a fireplace may keep you warm and comforted but does not mean you are lightened up inside of you. The fireplace light doesn't penetrate into your soul. It doesn't warm up your spirit neither brings comfort into your inner person. But the True Light has the power to transform you from inside out when you allow Him.

Your home may be furnished with expensive sophisticated lights and the most advance fire place but without the True Light of the world in you, you're still in darkness. Only the life of Jesus can give you permanent light for free yet very costly. *It cost His life to give you His Light.*

❧❧❧

# "It cost His life to give you His Light."

### Francis Herras

❧❧❧

Jesus said it clearly, *"Whoever <u>follows me</u> will never walk in darkness, but will have the light of life" (John 12:8 ESV, emphasis mine).*

*Jesus is the true Light of life.* He is the Light that penetrates into your innermost being, your spirit, soul and mind. Jesus' light will never dim and will never be dim by any form of darkness manifested through sins.

❧❧❧

# "Jesus is the true Light of life."

### Francis Herras

❧❧❧

The secret of walking in the light is following Jesus; meaning believing in Jesus as the true Light of your life; inviting Him into your life and making Him your personal Lord and Savior. When you do that the Holy Spirit comes and dwells in you and His light shines in you, upon you and through you.

Jesus light can never be dim by any form of darkness. Once Jesus is in you His life gives you light, shines in and through you. He is the Light you and I need today in this darkened world. Jesus is the Light the world needs to have and experience, Jesus Himself the true Light.

True light comes and shines through Jesus. Jesus light will transform your life you will never be the same again. Your exposure to Jesus' light is the beginning of you walking in His light. Following Jesus' teachings and principles is embracing His light. His words will enlighten your mind and feed your soul. Jesus is the Light of the world so let Him shine in your life, let Him shine in your home, marriage, family, business, work, church and communities.

Let Jesus' light shines in you and through you today! Let your life be an instrument of His light. Like a flashlight in the hands of Jesus. Be the sun that shines upon Earth. Never turn off Jesus' light keeps it shining and let people around you attracted to Jesus' light that they may see His light through you.

## A. The Will to Carry Out God's Work

*"I have FOOD to eat that you do not know about"*
*(John 4:32 ESV, emphasis mine).*

*"My FOOD is to do THE WILL OF HIM who sent me and TO ACCOMPLISH HIS WORK. Do you not say, there are yet four months, then comes the harvest? Look, I tell you, lift up your eyes, and see that the fields are white for harvest. Already the one who reaps is receiving wages and gathering fruit of eternal life, so that sower and reaper may rejoice together. For here the saying holds true, 'One sows, and another reaps.' I sent you to reap that for which you did not labor. Others have labored, and you have entered into their labor" (John 4:34-38 ESV, emphasis mine).*

On this remarkable event Jesus knew *"he had to pass through Samaria.* So he came to a town of Samaria called Sychar, near the field that Jacob had given to his son Joseph. Jacob's well was there; so Jesus, wearied as he was from his journey, was sitting beside the well. It was about the sixth hour" (John 4:-4-6 ESV).

I am in the point of view that Jesus did not accidentally arrive at Sychar by Jacob's well. Jesus saw *where* to go. He strategically placed himself with eager expectation of the coming Samaritan woman while his disciples left to buy food. I want you to bear in mind two concepts to learn from his meeting with the Samaritan woman.

First, Jesus used Jacob's well to attest He is the true Source of eternal life. Second, Jesus used the act of the disciples as parallel to communicate urgency to prioritized God's work.

Jesus did not stop the disciple from buying food. Food was a vital necessity. But, to shop for food was not Jesus top priority that moment. On the top of his agenda was "the *will of him who sent me and to accomplish his work*" (John 4:34 ESV). *Carrying out the Father's business was Jesus priority.* Jesus did not raise objections to the plan to buy food. But, had he joint his disciples to buy food he could have missed the work of the Father he was sent in to do particularly that day. For Jesus accomplishing the Father's will was his legitimate food which the disciples struggle to pay attention and comprehend.

ℒℒℒ

## "Carrying out the Father's business was Jesus priority."

### Francis Herras

ℒℒℒ

Food you can always have but seizing God-given opportunity for that particular time frame was crucial for the salvation of the Samaritan woman that has been instrumental to lead her city to listen to Jesus good news of salvation. Had Jesus made food his priority he could have missed *the appointed time of soul harvest for the Samaritans,* but *Jesus was aware of his priority—the harvest of souls!* Jesus was willing to be hungry for the redemption of the Samaritans. The disciple's priority was to buy food for everyone.

According to John 4:39-41, *"Many of the Samaritans from that town believed in him because of the woman's testimony"* (v.39a ESV). *"He told me everything I ever did"* (v.39b ESV). *"So when the Samaritans came to him, they urged him to stay with them, he stayed two days. And because of his words many more became believers"* (v.40c ESV).

75

In application, I am in my honest opinion that Jesus was teaching his disciples and us the 21ˢᵗ century believers to reexamine our preferences and choices doing God's work when occasion offers itself. *Jesus taught us the benefits of embracing God-made opportunity for a harvest of souls.* For Jesus, salvation of souls is always a priority over food when opportunity calls for it. Doing God's will in any given time of the day must be our top priority as Christ follower. *Doing the work of the Father is the real food of every Christian soul. Salvation is the real food one lost soul could ever have the rest of his earthly life.*

.ℰ.ℰ.ℰ

# "Jesus taught us the benefits of embracing God-made opportunity for a harvest of souls."

### Francis Herras

.ℰ.ℰ.

Whatever God-made opportunities before your eyes at this moment don't avoid it. Seize it! Pursue it. A bit of sacrifice won't harm you. Stick with it until everything is carried out so. In Jesus case, he waited by the well for the Samaritan woman and stay with her until she is saved. Then Jesus remained for two days longer with the Samaritans teach them the good news of the kingdom as a result *"many more believed because of his word" (John 4:41 ESV). Hopefully, you and I today learned this important lesson on urgency of carrying out God's work on time.*

Wherever you are at this moment, you are strategically positioned in the harvest field to introduce people to Christ for eternal life he offers to everyone.

## B. Uplifting and Discouraging Surprises

God uses ordinary people to encourage your heart. The reality of life at workplace environment is full of many unexpected surprises. Many of them are good and uplifting others are discouraging surprises. It looks 'uplifting and discouraging' surprises goes hand in hand waiting for the perfect day and time to manifest. When they arise people are affected on every level of their being may it be at home, at work, at church or wherever you are. The irony is you'll never know when those surprises are going to happen that's why we called them surprises. They just showed up without notice.

Let me give you a perfect example of what I mean by *'uplifting surprises.'* This happened to me personally. Looking back, I realize it was a simple practical way of God encouraging me because of the transition and challenges my family was going through at that time. It's been tough two years for me and my family. Transition is never been easy. When you are in those pressing moment 'uplifting surprise' makes you valued.

At work, Fridays I normally start to work at 7:00 in the morning. The reason is so I could go home by 3:00 in the afternoon because of the two-and-a-half hours drive home to be with my family before supper.

Another reason is my safety especially during winter. I prefer driving in daylight where I can clearly see the road and signs than driving when it's dark as you know 4:00 PM in winter is somewhat dark. If I leave work at 5:00 in the afternoon, it's dark, and difficult to drive for two-and-a-half hours sometime three hours especially when it's snowing or when it's foggy.

Going to work early on Fridays is a stretch because this means getting up at 5:00 early in the morning; driving for 5 hours weekly was a huge undertaking; worst was being away from my family 5 days a week while working. So hearing an 'uplifting surprise' in an environment where people don't showed to care enough is encouraging.

When you are in this kind of setting, I've just described you'll understand the feeling when someone asked you this question, *"Francis, how would you like to have a toast and egg before you start working, I know what being away from your family."* So I replied, "You know what, you are the only person who asked me that question and empathize in this environment we're in, you made my day today." She smiled and said, "Here, have a sit and eat." But I told her, "I'll take the food and eat my breakfast in my office."

I'm telling you it was the most delicious breakfast I've ever had. You know why, because of the thought behind it, the empathy, care and love behind that food offered to me. I felt so encouraged that morning. My spirit was uplifted and happy. I was nourished not only by the food she offered but nourished emotionally by her thoughts in my challenging circumstance. I wish more people like her at workplace!

Let me share with you statements shared with me from several employees at work just to give you an idea of the environment I describe:

> "I've been here for a long time but I have not received even one thank you."

> "Just wait, you'll understand, no one cares what you do. No one is doing right."

> "I've worked here for 10 years but not connected."

As I listened to those statements, I realized a missing part at work—affirmations, words of encouragement, or uplifting surprises. *The need for uplifting surprises from the leadership and management at workplace is obvious.* Employees at work are longing for something truthful, authentic, uplifting, positive words of encouragement.

Going back to my point, employees at work anywhere needs uplifting surprises than discouraging surprises as work itself is challenging. The reality of discouraging surprises intentionally designed waiting for a perfect time to come after you with hidden motives. But I guess we need both experience to grow, mature in relationship, empathy, listening, sensitivity, compassion and care. *The truth is people hurt people. Hurt people will hurt people. Encouraged people encourage other people as well.*

᎐᎐᎐

## "The truth is people hurt people. Hurt people will hurt people. Encouraged people encourage other People as well."

**Francis Herras**

᎐᎐᎐

*Opportunities and difficulties are twin realities of life everyone will have to go through no matter how godly you are.* There are rainy days and sunny days; both are essential ingredients of life. There are days hail storm may hit your crops just before harvest, a hard and difficult reality for farmers to bear. Being laid off or fired from a job is another brutal, painful reality that thousands of people around the world faced. *Encouragement makes you feel loved when you are going through tough times in life.*

### C. Words and You: The Power and Impact of your Spoken Words

"But the *tongue* can no man tame; it is an unruly evil, full of deadly poison. Therewith *bless we God,* even the Father; and therewith *curse we men,* which are made after the similitude of God. *Out of the same mouth proceedeth blessing and cursing.* My brethren, these things ought not so to be. Doth a fountain send forth at the same place sweet water and bitter? Can the fig tree, my brethren, bear olive berries? Either a vine, figs? So can no fountain both yield salt water and fresh," (James 3:8-12 KJV, emphasis mine).

Was the apostle James telling us that the literal tongue is the problem here? Does human tongue voluntarily create words by itself? Does your tongue act independently from your mind? I'm sure James was not pointing out to a literal tongue but uses the human tongue as an analogy to communicate a message - *the power and impact of spoken words and what it does.*

Your tongue is a gift to you by God so you can speak and articulate ideas thoughts in an organized and coherent manner. The problem James was dealing with was the negativism and cursing in the Body of Christ in which according to James should never happen.

The tongue doesn't make up words to express by itself. *Words imply what's in the heart.* Words flow from the heart. Out of the plethora of the heart the mouth utters.

♪♪♪

# "Words imply what's in the heart."

### Francis Herras

♪♪♪

According to James, *words have weight*. Words can build and destroy life. *Words impact the innermost being of the person positively or negatively expressed. Every conversation you engage with your children will have immediate and lasting consequence and influence in their way of life and thought pattern.* Your words have the power to shape your marriage relationship and family dynamic. Words can build and destroy. It penetrates into the heart. This is why God put his Words (the Bible) into writing so we read and transform the state of our mind. The Bible is the Word of God that can regenerate your spirit and change your life.

꙳꙳꙳

# "Words impact the innermost being of the person positively or negatively expressed. Every conversation you engage with your children will have immediate and lasting consequence and influence in their way of life and thought pattern."

**Francis Herras**

꙳꙳꙳

With our tongue we *bless* God with the same tongue we *curse* others, made after the image of God. Why is this? In order to avoid this behavior **you must define the source of the uttered words first.** Where is the *spoken "blessing"* coming from and where is the *spoken "cursing"* coming? It comes from the same mouth of the same person. In order to *trace the source of spoken words* one must look deep into heart and mind of the one speaking. Spoken curse could potentially be coming from the *old sinful nature* triggered by pain, angered, jealousy, rivalry, hatred, want or greed. Spoken curses could come from the *mind of the flesh* part of the sinful nature. Spoken curses could mean *outside influence or satanic attack* to destroy your relationship with God, loved ones and friends. *You must name the source of your spoken words.*

## D. Two Possible Origins of Spoken Words

*Spoken words show its source. There are two possible sources of origin of spoken words. One is the Word of God, and second, is the world values.* Spoken words show the information stored in the heart. Spoken words show the state of the mind and the state of the heart of the person.

꙳꙳꙳

# "Spoken words show its source. There are two possible sources of origin of spoken words. One is the Word of God, and second, is the world values."

### Francis Herras

꙳꙳꙳

The truth is, your spoken words tell you who you are and the person you are becoming. Spoken words are not just words. They show who you are as a person, the quality of your spiritual life and your thought patterns.

*You are what you think. What you think is what you say. What you say comes from your heart who and what you are!*

Spoken words are window for people to peek into your heart. The more you talk the more you expose the content and state of your heart and mind. Spoken words give people around you a glimpse of what's going on inside of your heart and mind. *Words serve as a descriptor of the state of your thoughts, feelings, emotions and nature.* Spoken words tell the depths condition of your heart and relationships with other people. Your words show your personality, your perspective, perception and philosophy you embrace in life. *People around you will soon have a picture of who you are by just listening to your spoken words.*

♆♆♆

## "Words serve as a descriptor of the state of your thoughts, feelings, emotions and nature."

Francis Herras

♆♆♆

### E.  The Power of the Words

Your spoken words have the power to *attract people and attract opportunities* but it has the power to push people away and destroy opportunities. *Your spoken words are the seed that you sow for your future.* This is why you must listen carefully to every word that comes out of your mouth because once spoken you can't take them back it becomes the very intent it was spoken. *The power of the word is the intent behind it and the feelings and emotion behind that goes with it.* So words are not just words. It is loaded with intent, purpose, thoughts, motives, feelings that comes deep from the heart of the one who spoke them. Words encapsulate ideas; evoke emotion, personality, displays attitudes and characters of the person that spoke it. This is why you felt deeply the hurts of words spoken.

♆♆♆

## "The power of the word is the intent behind it and the feelings and emotion behind that goes with it."

Francis Herras

♆♆♆

Here is the question. *What kinds of words are coming out of your mouth now days?* Is it words of wisdom and life? Is it positive or negative words? Does your word build or does it destroy people? Do your words harmonize or does it disunite? Does it encourage or does it discourage people around you? Does your word attract people and opportunities or does it dispels them? Does it bless or does it curse? Are you aware of the words proceeding out of your mouth when you speak?

## F.   Words Reflects Belief System

> *"Do not labor for the food which perishes, but for the food which endures to everlasting life, which the Son of Man will give you, because God the Father has set His seal on Him"* (*John 6:27 NKJV*).

> *"This is the work of God, that you believe in Him whom He sent" (John 6:29 NKJV).*

> *"Then Jesus said to them, "Most assuredly, I say to you, Moses did not give you the bread from heaven, but My Father gives you the true bread from heaven. For the bread of God is He who comes down from heaven and gives life to the world"* (*John 6:32-33 NKJV*).

> *"And Jesus said to them, "I am the bread of life. He who comes to Me shall never hunger, and he who believes in Me shall never thirst" (John 6:35 NKJV).*

> *"Most assuredly, I say to you, he who believes in Me has everlasting life. I am the bread of life" (John 6:47-48 NKJV).*

> *"It is the Spirit who gives life; the flesh profits nothing. **The words that I speak** to you **are spirit**, and **they are life"*** (*John 6:63 NKJV, emphasis mine*).

> ***"The WORDS I have spoken to you are SPIRIT and LIFE"*** (*John 6:63 ESV, emphasis mine*).

*According to Jesus his spoken words are spirit and life.* People did not *literally* see the words Jesus has spoken they HEARD them. Words don't have shapes, colors, or body but power and life. *Jesus spoken words have power and life.* People felt the power, life and authority of Jesus' words when he teaches. Jesus words heal and save many lives. For those that believe Jesus, his words gave them life eternal but for those who did not believe him his words caused them to dissociate from him.

*Jesus words give life* because Jesus is the Life, the Author and Creator of life. True life only gives life. When he spoke he spoke life. He spoke life eternal. Believing Jesus' words gives you life and gives you eternal life.

*Jesus words gives life!* As Christians Jesus is our model in life. Listening closely to Jesus' words in the Bible will dramatically change our lifestyle, the way we talk with other people beginning in our own household. The more we listen to Jesus the more we learn the way he thinks, convey his message, ideas and thoughts to the surrounding people.

♪♪♪

# "As Christians Jesus is our model in life."

### Francis Herras

♪♪♪

*Jesus words attract people* then He points them to the Father. Isn't this a great example for us followers of Christ? *Do your words attract people or does it drive people away?* Does your word evoke power, authority and life or does it destroys or tears life? Have you ever listen closely to the words that come out of your mouth lately? Have you ever taken a serious assessment to every word that you have spoken or about to say? Have you thought through your words properly; the intent and motive behind your words; have you considered the impact of your words? Are your words designs to build life? Are your words evoked the power and authority of Christ?

As a Christian words of life should be natural evidence in our daily conversation because of the indwelling presence of Christ and the Holy Spirit that gives us the ability to choose what to say - words of life or words that kill. You have a choice where to draw your words—the mind of Christ or your own mind; the Word of God (Bible) or the world's value? Which source does your words comes? Does it come from the Word of God or does it comes from world's value (world's philosophies)? The source of your words, ideas, thoughts is crucial. The first source is God focus and gives life. The latter is self and worldly focused that kills.

*The source of your ideas and words are important.* If your ideas and values are coming from God's Word it will give you life and bring you closer to God and make you become the person God want you to be. If the source of your ideas and values are the world's value and philosophies, it will bring you closer to yourself, the world and become what the world wants you to become.

❧❧❧

## "Your life reflects the source of your words, ideas, values and philosophies."

### Francis Herras

❧❧❧

What you are becoming is absolutely a product of the belief that you've embraced. *Your life reflects the source of your words, ideas, values and philosophies.* The words you speak and say are reflections of your belief and the very source of that belief. It is easy to notice the belief people have because of their lifestyle, expressed ideas, priorities in life, relationships they engaged in, the way they see things and people they associate. Your words show where your drawing them a mirror of what is stored in your heart. Out of the abundance of the heart the mouth speaks according to Jesus.

Negative people speak negative words. Mockers speak to mock. What can you expect from them but to express what's in their mind and the belief they embraced? Belief creates life style this idea is essential to look deep into the sources of what you believe and why you believe them. Why is this important? It is important because you live out your belief. Your life will be driven by what you believe regardless of its source.

♪♪♪

# "Your life will be driven by what you believe regardless of its source."

**Francis Herras**

♪♪♪

One way to examine your belief is asked these questions? Is my belief producing me a godly life? Is my belief drawing closer to God? Am I becoming a better person because of my belief? Do I speak words of life, peace, joy, love, unity, comfort, blessings and healing? What kinds of words are coming out of your mouth, are they good words, are they positive words, or are they negative and destructive words and where are those words arising from and why? The apostle James exhorts us "to be *quick* to HEAR, *slow* to SPEAK" (James 1:19 ESV, emphasis mine).

## G. What is Belief?

What is belief? What does it do? How does it affect our thinking, behavior, lifestyle and work habit? How do we know we are operating in beliefs that are not helping us? Where does belief originated? How does it develop? Are there identifiable contributing factors to the development of our belief? Do our current lifestyle, work style, leadership style, personality, relationships, values and philosophies show our belief?

*Is belief a system?* What forms it? What drives it? What fuels it? How do we develop healthy belief? Where do we start? Where do we begin discovering our personal belief and creating new healthy belief to replace old belief that doesn't work for us or doesn't help us but hinders or pull us to move forward according to what you think God has prepared for your future? So, where do we begin in our journey in the realm of belief?

☙☙☙

# "The bottom line is to know yourself you must know your beginning. You must treasure your origin."

## Francis Herras

☙☙☙

I suggest that we begin our belief journey with God in Genesis *"In the beginning God"* (Genesis 1:1 NKJV). This idea is the most logical and moral thing to do. Recognizing and acknowledging God the cause of *"the beginning"* is a moral act that superlatively honor God, give Him due credit and love in a way that you acknowledge and recognize your parents, respect your parents and love your parents that birthed you to life. *The bottom line is to know yourself you must know your beginning. You must treasure your origin.* Tracing back where you came from is an essential contributing part to understanding your present belief.

There are two primary sources foundational to belief that I want to discuss.

1. God our heavenly Father
2. Our earthly parents

Let me begin by saying God is the Foundation of the universe. The entire creation came from the holy mind of God. Everything was 'conceived' in the sovereign compassionate heart of God. He caused the entire creation including the first human being Adam. Creation is and will always be founded on who God is and is and will always be sustained by God including the human race beginning from Adam until now.

We must realize that it was the life that comes from God that makes the first man and humanity today become a living soul. In the same manner the life from God will sustain followers of Christ throughout eternity. Man is a product of the Triune God's eternal decision. Man was not made out of nowhere. Man was made with meticulous planning, consultation and deliberation within a perfect loving Triune God. *"Then God said, "Let **Us** make man in **Our** image, according to **Our** likeness" (Genesis 1:26 NKJV,* *emphasis mine).* There was no room for error when the Triune God made the decision to create man. God himself is 'the pattern' of creating man. This makes man originated from God.

Then God said, *"Let us make mankind in our image, in our likeness, so that they may rule over the fish in the sea and the birds in the sky, over the livestock and all the wild animals and over all the creatures that move along the ground"* (Genesis 1:26 NIV).

The very first thing that Adam sees when he opens his eyes and become a living soul was his Creator, God Himself his Father.

I believe the formation of Adam's belief was when God was creating him. Everything God wants for Adam was embedded in his DNA creation. Everything he needed in life was encapsulated when God breath the breath of life upon him. Adam knew as part of his design that he was created and originated from God. I'm sure God took time to nourish, loved, equipped, and prepared Adam for what lies ahead of him. Adam was aware of who God is. He knew God's voice. He hears God's voice. God was his Father.

- Hearing God's voice
- Feeling God's love
- Aware of God's presence his Father
- Abundantly provided with everything he needed to live
- Perfect climate, a perfect home, perfect Father
- Perfect wife

*I believe Adam's relationship and conversation with God was the primary source of his personal development in the Garden. Adam's belief system originated and developed in the Garden of Eden his home in relationship with God the Father.*

- His belief about his origin
- His belief about who he is
- His belief about relationships
- His belief about marriage
- His belief about home
- His belief about his family and children
- His belief about provisions

- His belief about work
- His belief about life and living
- His belief about God's plan (his Father)
- His belief about future (for sure God spoke to him about his future)
- His belief about God's moral law
- His belief about love and obedience
- His belief about creation the universe
- His belief about environment
- His belief about nature
- His belief about natural resources
- His belief about living creatures

*The above evolved and develop in Adam's walk with God.* Suffice to say on this premise that the formation of Adam's belief system was created progressively within a relationship with God in his home Garden of Eden Paradise. It is in the Paradise that everything happens. *The foundation of civilized and true belief is God himself.* I think this idea the safest and highest form of moral, relational, spiritual, social, familial and environmental belief to name a few, we could learn and emulate in our belief system today. *There at the Garden happens the transference of God's worldview to Adam.* I believe Adam learned to see things the way God see things. God's worldview and perspective was transferred and embedded in Adam thus to the entire human race on planet earth by virtue of racial origin.

❧❧❧

# "The foundation of civilized and true belief is God himself."

## Francis Herras

❧❧❧

## H. How Belief Work

Our Beliefs is influence and affected by our *life's experience*. Adam and Eve formation of belief was influenced by their daily *experience* with *God*, the *environment* where God place them, their *relational dynamics* with each other as a couple, the *work* they were assigned to do, but more importantly how God present Himself to the couple as their heavenly Father and sovereign Creator of the universe.

There are two essential things that play an important role on the change in the belief. *One is the **individual person** responding or creating his environment. The other one is, **the environment** impacting the individual person's daily experience.* This real experience is processed and filtered by the conscious mind and then the preferred impact of the experience is stored in the subconscious mind ultimately becomes a part of the *web belief framework*. That newly formed web of belief is solidified by two things—by *reasons* interpretation/perception/knowledge) and empirical *experience*. Reasons are that *empirical* knowledge behind the experience. Actual experiences are those experience acted upon driven by reasons.

Belief must have a *context* or *setting*. Adam and Eve belief was formed and developed within *the context of God's governance* before the fall. God's governing laws and principles are reasons that are part of their daily experience in Eden that drives them how they respond to one another and their environment entrusted by God. As Adam and Eve progress in their knowledge their individual experiences progress. Thus both *their individual belief constantly change within the context of their relationship with God's Theocratic governance.*

Let me show you how belief develops by using the spider web analogy. Let me illustrate further for clarity sake.

# Belief System

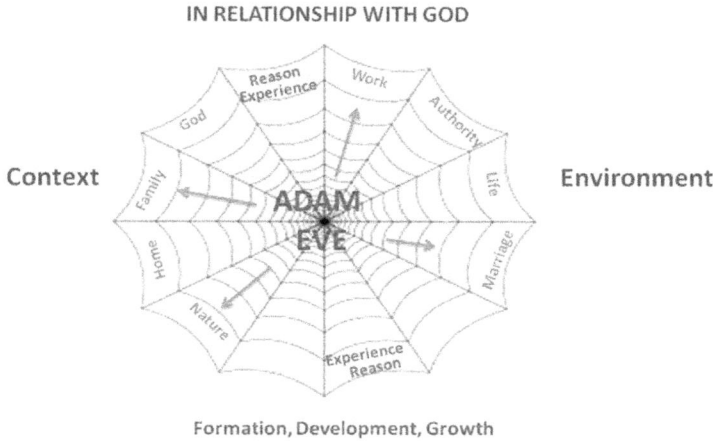

IN RELATIONSHIP WITH GOD

Context

Environment

ADAM EVE

Formation, Development, Growth

*Belief systems are structures of norms that you have developed overtime by reason and experience.* But not every norm you've collected and embedded in your subconscious mind are helping you become the person God want you to be. Many of those norms you've gathered from conception are causes of failure in your life, ministry, work, and or has been contributing factors that have created a lifestyle without reference to God. This is why extremely important for you and me to revisit and examine thoroughly the layers of your personal belief you've structured deep in your sub-conscious mind unconsciously by reason and by experience.

༄༄༄

## "Belief systems are structures of norms that you have developed overtime by reason and experience."

### Francis Herras

༄༄༄

You must do an *autopsy* on your belief. Did you design a belief that is founded in the Person of God? Is the object of your belief the Creator of the universe? Did you structure your belief in such a way that it honors God? Is God at the core of your belief? Is your belief elevates that sanctity of life? Do you embrace a belief that preserves the true meaning of family and marriage as design by God stipulated in the Bible? What belief have you developed? Have you developed a Christ-centered belief? Or have you developed a humanistic and secularist belief that opposes or contradict the universal moral principles laid by God in His Word – the Bible?

Why is it important to examine our belief? *It is extremely essential to examine our belief because it has the power to govern our behaviors.* Listen and observed the paragraph below that tackles the distinction between rules, norms, and belief. But, I focus my attention more on beliefs on number three.

> "Strategic approaches make a distinction between rules, norms and beliefs as follows: (1) Rules. Explicit regulative processes such as policies, laws, inspection routines, or incentives. Rules function as a coercive regulator of behavior and are dependent upon the imposing entity's ability to enforce them. (2) Norms. Regulative mechanisms accepted by the social collective. Norms are enforced by normative mechanisms within the organization and are not strictly dependent upon law or regulation. (3) Beliefs. The collective perception of fundamental truths governing behavior. The adherence to accepted and shared beliefs by members of a social system will likely persist and be difficult to change over time. Strong beliefs about determinant factors (i.e., security, survival, or honor) are likely to cause a social entity or group to accept rules and norms."[56]

Number three tells us, "Belief is the collective perception of fundamental truths governing behaviors." My issue with this idea is the

---

[56] Chairman of the Joint Chiefs of Staff, U.S. Army (2012). Information Operations. Joint Publication 3-13. Joint Doctrine Support Division, 116 Lake View Parkway, Suffolk, VA. p. 22.

basis of the "fundamental truths" and how that "truths" is perceived and define. Are those "fundamental truths" conducive to the moral absolute truth of God in Scripture? Are those "collective perception" developed within a relational context with the highest form of Intelligence in the universe—God? "Collective perception of fundamental truths governing behaviors" must be measured by the absolute truth of God. Fundamental truths must be measured by God's absolute truth.

### Belief Development Process

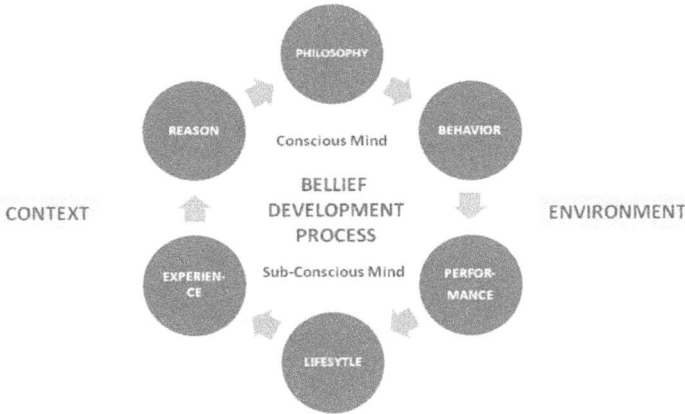

**Belief Development Process**

PHILOSOPHY

REASON    BEHAVIOR

Conscious Mind

CONTEXT    BELLIEF DEVELOPMENT PROCESS    ENVIRONMENT

EXPERIEN-CE    Sub-Conscious Mind    PERFOR-MANCE

LIFESYTLE

## I.  The Gospel and Compassionate Acts Order of Priority

*Embracing God's wisdom and His Words is the key to wise and dynamic belief system and living.* The book of Proverbs tells us, the fear of the Lord is the beginning of wisdom. It is the wisdom that comes from the "fear of the Lord" arising from *reverence* based on who God is—his nature and attributes. It is the *wisdom that comes from a regenerated heart and a renewed mind.* It is the wisdom that embraces the importance and essential value of a relationship with God through Christ Jesus. It is the wisdom that generates a lifestyle that embraces and propagates the priorities of the Kingdom of God here on earth.

Here is what I think are the Priorities of the Kingdom of God:

1. The GOSPEL of the Kingdom (*proclamation*)
2. The COMPASSIONATE ACTS of the Kingdom (*practice*)
3. The PRINCIPLES of the Kingdom (*discipleship*)
4. The LIFESTYLE of the Kingdom (*church*)

Compassionate acts alone are not the goal of God's Kingdom. When Jesus came on earth for his redemptive work his lifestyle oozes and displays without shortage of compassionate acts, but we must realize and put things in right perspective that his utmost and highest priority is the proclamation of the "good news of the kingdom" or "good news of salvation of the kingdom" for the redemption of depraved and fallen humanity and the system they embraced.

The challenge with 21ˢᵗ century Christianity is doing compassionate acts without the *"gospel of salvation"* although interpreted as Christian faith-based organization it doesn't show the priority of the kingdom of God which was presented and modeled by Jesus Christ.

*Compassionate acts, as good as they are, they are not the prevailing kingdom priority.* God's compassion reflects the preeminence of Christ redemptive priority "to seek and save the lost" rebellious humanity. Jesus redemptive acts embodied the ultimate act of compassion; the motif of his work was "to save and seek the lost" first and foremost.

Divine love and compassion was the motive within the Triune God that Jesus Christ the second person of the Trinity lovingly offered his precious life for the redemption of mankind (John 3:16) including the system they're enslaved. *Compassionate acts are good when done in connection with the first motif otherwise plainly good works with ulterior agenda, not kingdom centered and Christ-centered and not operating according to Christ priorities to seek and save the lost.*

## Compassionate Acts in Health Care Setting

Compassionate acts done within the health care setting such as in nursing homes, hospice, social services, and among many so-called faith-based charitable organizations that provides care services are *humanitarian care services focused driven for profit.* Although they are helpful and essential social services that cater to the various needs of the people in society, but, they are not kingdom oriented or Christ centered organization driven but by *humanitarian programs* in most cases motivated by self interest, corporate agenda or organization's so-called mission, purpose and values which does not show God's Kingdom agenda to seek and save the lost from the bondage of sins and from the system of this fallen world.

Most of these organizations define compassionate acts according to their corporate philosophy, a purpose and a mission to generate revenue or advance their religion far remote from Christ redemptive motif which defines what compassionate acts within kerygmatic mindset or kingdom agenda.

## J. Things are Moving Forward

Things are moving forward! When I embarked in the position as a business counselor in a financial company I have three things in mind - to SEEK, SAVE AND SERVE the lost. This is the mindset and belief that I embrace. *To seek, save, and serve the lost corporate world; to seek, save, and serve the hurting professionals out there in the corporate world by pointing them to Jesus Christ;* give them hope to awaken their dreams and potentials to fulfill God's design for their lives.

I am so grateful working closer with my family. Thing happens for a reason. That reason is unfolding before my eyes. I think God has strategically positioned me at my current work to hone my counseling, coaching, and leadership skills among the professional in the financial industry. I believe God put me here to serve his purpose.

I believe by doing so I will be rewarded greatly and my family needs will be exceedingly provided more than I could ever ask or imagined. I am thankful for the opportunity at this moment that I can plant seeds of success among the financial advisors in Calgary. So far I am enjoying teaching, coaching, counseling and providing lectures on Personal Development Training. It feels good to see people being educated, challenge, and pointed to God their Creator. It gives me a good feeling when advisors come to me after my talk and extend their hands and say, "thank you Francis," "wow you're so good" or "I've learned so much," "I'm glad I came," "your call pays off," etc. I see these as affirmations to what I am now doing - fulfilling Gods design for my life.

Great things happen since I came back from Lethbridge to Calgary! I do believe I was providentially positioned where I am. My wife Evelyn shows interest in the financial industry business she attends Tuesday training; I was able to create Professional Care Counseling Program for the company; present lecture every Tuesday among Calgary advisors, regular meeting with Business Development Manager to brainstorm and do strategic planning for the next step to move the company forward. The regular workshop was amazing. Even though it's only my first month in the position as business counselor yet great results are happening. Advisors are enthusiastic and excited. Tuesday Business Development Meeting attendance has increased reasonably. Our Calgary office is alive! I am grateful to be instrumental for the positive change and momentum taking place in Calgary office!

The good thing is I am closer to home my family doing what I love to do. I don't have to travel 5 or 6 hours a week, pay $1200 a month rent, 5 days away from my family a week, being alone, incur gas expense, etc. I am backed home, blessed and positioned by God into the next level of my purpose! I am where I am because God has prepared me perfectly for this season of my life.

## K. Developing Healthy Emotion and Thought Pattern

How do you develop healthy emotion and thought pattern?

First, *discipline* yourself to *develop a deeper level of awareness* of your emotion and thought realm. This is a skill everyone must develop. You must be mindful of every particular feelings and thoughts that arise within you then look at it, examine it and ask, where is this feeling or thought coming from and why? How did it impact your behaviors, performance and lifestyle?

Second, *name* your triggers.

What triggers or cause those feelings and thoughts. There are so many possible triggers. What are the circumstances surrounding it? How should you handle and response with your own thoughts and feelings both positive and negative?

## L.  The Importance of Developing a Deeper Level of Self-Awareness

Why is it important to cultivate a *deeper sense of awareness*? Cultivating a deeper awareness is important because our *"thoughts and feelings"* affect our behavior, response, perspective, performance, relationships, health, lifestyle and decision making. This is why it's important to develop a discipline of awareness or *connectedness with your emotional and thoughts dynamic pattern* to do necessary adjustment or correction needed to develop a healthy emotion and thought pattern as you move forward accomplishing your purpose in life.

*Discovering healthy ways conducive to the Scripture to discuss your emotional and thought pattern challenges is essential to your personal or professional progress.* You must be willing to name emotions and thoughts that affect your behaviors significantly or cause damage to your personality and lifestyle.

꒰꒱꒲

## "Discovering healthy ways conducive to the Scripture to discuss your emotional and thought pattern challenges is essential to your personal or professional progress."

### Francis Herras

꒰꒱꒲

The key to healthy emotion and thought pattern is developing a deeper awareness of yourself; *develop a practice of connecting with your emotional and thought realm* and be able to find areas where correction or development is needed and then discover the *root cause* behind those negative feelings and thoughts and then *replace* them with a healthy one.

*Your emotion and thought world is connected to your five senses.* These realms are interconnected and inter-related in nature. The five senses influence the emotion and thought and vise versa. You cannot decompartmentalize yourself. *Your whole being is interconnected spiritually, psychologically and physiologically. Each affects the other one.*

Let me give you an example. An aroma of coffee triggers a thought to drink coffee. A smell of roasted beef triggers hungers, and a thought to eat.

ℒℒℒ

## "Your whole being is interconnected spiritually, psychologically and physiologically. Each affects the other one."

### Francis Herras

ℒℒℒ

Feeling is an emotion which affects your thoughts. A severe back pain and headache will definitely affect the state of your thought pattern thus your perspective in so many ways. On the other hand peaceful, joyful and happy experience will affect your thought pattern thus your perspective. The key to developing a healthy emotion and thought pattern is to understand the impact and effect of those experiences that triggers those thoughts and feelings and ask why.

- Why is this happening to me?
- How did I land on this mindset?
- Who and what causes it?
- What or who triggers my thoughts and feelings?
- What behaviors this generated?
- How is this affecting me?
- Is this helping me?

Once you have gathered correct facts of information surrounding your experience, you can now *act upon to manage your emotion and thoughts*, fine tune, do a necessary reconstruction to your growth and progress to become the person you wish to become.

*You must be aware that your physiological senses affect your psychological senses which impact your spiritual senses.* Spirit, soul and body dynamics are interconnected with each other. These three spheres are inseparable. The context of your experience will impact your emotional and thought pattern. The key is to discover and understand yourself how you react and response to those experiences that triggers specifically negative feelings and thoughts then manage them to replace them with positive and healthy ideas to develop positive strong mindset.

## M. Work Hard on Yourself

Healthy emotion and positive thought pattern don't just happen. You must constantly work hard on yourself to become a better person. You must work hard on every areas of your being to become successful in life. *The better person you become the more valuable you become with your family, business and organization. So if you want more success you must work hard on yourself in developing healthy mindset and emotions that will lead you to a view from the top.* The more you become better in your thoughts and heart the more you climb spiritually and the more you climb your view change and becomes wider and better. The more you become valuable to God's Kingdom, others and yourself the more God exalts you. *The way to the view from the top is keep working hard on you in humility in relationship with Christ.*

.º.º.º.

## "The way to the view from the top is keep working hard on you in humility in relationship with Christ."

**Francis Herras**

.º.º.º.

## UPWARD MOMENTUM ACTION STAPS

*Write your answers on a clean sheet of paper.*

How do you subdued "old sinful nature," "earthly mindset," or "worldly pattern," lifestyle?

How do you live a crucified life, a fully surrendered life?

How do you apply Jesus' words in your daily life, "Whoever <u>follows me</u> will not walk in darkness, but will have <u>the light of life</u>" (John 8:12 ESV)

The harvest of souls is the priority of God's Kingdom on earth. Are you involved in the harvest of soul? Why not?

Can you give a personal example of the power and impact of spoken words and what it does to you?

Describe your own belief system and its formation.

How is your belief making you?

# CHAPTER 9

# Humility Recognizes God is Greater

*"Because your heart was tender and you humbled yourself before God when you heard His words against this place and against its inhabitants, and because you humbled yourself before Me, tore your clothes and wept before Me, I truly have heard you," declares the LORD."*
*(2 Chronicles 34:27 ESV)*

*Humble people recognized God is greater!* They acknowledge He is the absolute greatness. Humble people acknowledge true greatness comes from God. Humble people embrace the philosophy that says no greatness apart from God far greater and more than greater than any great things in universe man attributes. God is beyond description, indescribable and unfathomable in every way, his nature and attributes.

*The languages of the earth will not be enough even to describe the greatness of His holiness, purity and power.* Man's language is limited to the person speaking, describing and perceiving God thus finite in every way of its conception and understanding of God who caused the universe into existence totally dependent upon his providence.

*God is greater than his creation.* He is greater than his works though his works displays the splendor of his great power, wisdom and knowledge. His greatness is seen in the order and preservation of the universe. God's greatness of intelligence and wisdom is seen in the uniqueness of the four seasons, the continuous multiplication of various living species on earth—the fishes of the sea, the birds of the air, the beasts of the forest and the mountains; God's greatness is displayed in His design of the different seeds that produces different kinds of fruits, crops or vegetable. These are just a few examples of God's greatness.

*The closer you walk with God, the closer you see a glimpse of the view from the top. Your pursuit of God is your way up to the view from the top.*

Remember the story of Moses when he pursues God in the wilderness at Mount Horeb in the burning Bush? For me, *Moses experience at Mount Horeb in God's holy presence is a perfect example of a view from the top!* Moses personal encounter with God totally transformed him from inside out as an individual. God spoke to him in the burning Bush. God calls him to a mission to set the Hebrew people free from the bondage of Pharaoh in Egypt so they can become a nation under God. A nation made by God for God to serve His purpose.

***

# "The closer you walk with God, the closer you see a glimpse of the view from the top. Your pursuit of God is your way up to the view from the top."

**Francis Herras**

***

Let's revisit Moses experience at the burning Bush at Mount Horeb to show you what I mean when I say a view from the top. Open your Bible in Exodus chapter 3:1-22.

> "Now Moses was tending the flock of Jethro his father-in-law, the priest of Midian. And he led the flock to the back of the desert, and came to **Horeb, the mountain of God**. ² And *the Angel of the Lord appeared to him in a flame of fire from the midst of a bush. So he looked, and behold, the bush was burning with fire, but the bush was not*

*consumed.* ³ Then Moses said, "I will now turn aside and see this great sight, why the bush does not burn."

⁴ So when the Lord saw that he turned aside to look, *God called to him* from the midst of the bush and said, "Moses, Moses!"

And he said, "Here I am."

⁵ Then He said, "Do not draw near this place. Take your sandals off your feet, for the place where you stand *is* holy ground." ⁶ Moreover He said, "I *am* the God of your father—the God of Abraham, the God of Isaac, and the God of Jacob." And Moses hid his face, for he was afraid to look upon God.

⁷ And the Lord said: "I have surely seen the oppression of My people who *are* in Egypt, and have heard their cry because of their taskmasters, for I know their sorrows. ⁸ So *I have come down to deliver them out of the hand of the Egyptians, and to bring them up from that land to a good and large land, to a land flowing with milk and honey,* to the place of the Canaanites and the Hittites and the Amorites and the Perizzites and the Hivites and the Jebusites. ⁹ Now therefore, behold, the cry of the children of Israel has come to Me, and I have also seen the oppression with which the Egyptians oppress them. ¹⁰ ***Come now, therefore, and I will send you to Pharaoh that you may bring My people, the children of Israel, out of Egypt.***"

¹¹ But Moses said to God, "Who *am* I that I should go to Pharaoh, and that I should bring the children of Israel out of Egypt?"

¹² So He said, "*I will certainly be with you.* And this *shall be* a sign to you that *I have sent you*: When you have

brought the people out of Egypt, *you shall serve God on this mountain*."

13 Then Moses said to God, "Indeed, *when* I come to the children of Israel and say to them, 'The God of your fathers has sent me to you,' and they say to me, 'What *is* His name?' what shall I say to them?"

14 And God said to Moses, "I AM WHO I AM." And He said, "Thus you shall say to the children of Israel, 'I AM has sent me to you.'" 15 Moreover God said to Moses, "Thus you shall say to the children of Israel: 'The Lord God of your fathers, the God of Abraham, the God of Isaac, and the God of Jacob, has sent me to you. This *is* My name forever, and this *is* My memorial to all generations.' 16 Go and gather the elders of Israel together, and say to them, 'The Lord God of your fathers, the God of Abraham, of Isaac, and of Jacob, appeared to me, saying, "I have surely visited you and *seen* what is done to you in Egypt; 17 and I have said I will bring you up out of the affliction of Egypt to the land of the Canaanites and the Hittites and the Amorites and the Perizzites and the Hivites and the Jebusites, to a land flowing with milk and honey."' 18 Then they will heed your voice; and you shall come, you and the elders of Israel, to the king of Egypt; and you shall say to him, 'The Lord God of the Hebrews has met with us; and now, please, let us go three days' journey into the wilderness, that we may sacrifice to the Lord our God.' 19 But I am sure that the king of Egypt will not let you go, no, not even by a mighty hand. 20 So I will stretch out My hand and strike Egypt with all My wonders which I will do in its midst; and after that he will let you go. 21 And I will give this people favor in the sight of the Egyptians; and it shall be, when you go, that you shall not go empty-handed. 22 But every woman shall ask of her neighbor, namely, of her who dwells near her

house, articles of silver, articles of gold, and clothing; and you shall put *them* on your sons and on your daughters. So you shall plunder the Egyptians." (Exodus 3:1-22 NKJV)

What an invitation to Moses by God to *work* with Him, "***Come now, therefore, and I will send you to Pharaoh that you may bring My people, the children of Israel, out of Egypt***" (Exodus 3:10 NKJV, emphasis mine). God was *hiring* Moses' to work with Him to lead and manage the Hebrew exit from Egypt. What a view from the top!

It was at Mount Horeb God hired Moses to work with Him. Moses life was totally changed by God's calling. *What a paradigm shift of perspective and agenda on Moses part—a calling to work with God to advance His Kingdom agenda on earth in Egypt.* What a huge responsibility at the same time a privilege to represent God backing him up to carry out his mandate. *The view from the top totally alters the destiny of Moses' life and the Hebrew people chosen and loved by God.* Indeed, the view from the top totally transformed Moses from inside out. *He was captivated by God and His mandate.* Moses was never been the same again.

The Scripture tells me that when Moses saw the burning bush; he came closer and responded. As a result, he had a life-changing encounter with God his Maker. Moses experience with God not only transformed his life but delivers the lives of the Hebrew people from bondage of slavery into God's promise land. ***It was in the presence of God that Moses views become clearer:***

- *His view of God*
- *His view of God's call*
- *His view of himself*
- *His view of the Hebrew people and needs*
- *His view of the Egyptian*
- *His view of God's plan and purpose*

In short, ***Moses view was elevated to God's view.*** Moses perspective was changed to God's perspective. He sees what God sees. When God showed him His plan and entrusted this plan to him, Moses *worldview* of Egypt and the Hebrew people was changed. ***I call Moses experienced***

**with God in the burning bush a view from the top experience. Seeing what God sees is the best panoramic view from the top that Moses embraced!**

The question is what do you see? Whose lens do you see through your life purpose, marriage, family, work and ministry call? What is your view of God? Who is He to your existence here on earth? Below are views you may want to embrace and incorporate in your personal belief structure.

♪♪♪

## "I call Moses experienced with God in the burning bush a view from the top experience. Seeing what God sees is the best panoramic view from the top that Moses embraced!"

### Francis Herras

♪♪♪

*God is the author of life.* "For in him we live and move and exist …" (Acts 17:28 LEB). What makes you absolutely different from animals is the image and likeness of God in you. This is the true life that God breadth upon you and caused you into existence became living intelligent creature. *Apart from God you have no life because God is the cause, the source, the definition and ultimate meaning of life.* You and I are neatly designed by the author of life. Every significant parts of your body are delicately designed of God. Your existence on earth is willed by God. Your presence on this planet is valued by God who sent his Son Jesus Christ to redeem you from bondage and oppression of sin. Jesus gave his life, shed his blood for people of the world to be saved and enjoy the more abundant life he offers! Jesus came so you may have life more abundantly. Jesus claimed, *"I am the resurrection and the life. The one who believes in me, even if he dies, will live"* *(John 11:25 LEB).* Your life apart from Jesus is just existence but your life in Jesus is the true life that has been restored into the image and likeness of God. Christ came to make you whole by giving you his life in exchange for your "sinful life," or "earthly life style" so that his life flourish in and through you and you become the person he desired for you to become. So the idea of life outside of God is far remote from the truth.

ℰℰℰ

## "Apart from God you have no life because God is the cause, the source, the definition and ultimate meaning of life."

### Francis Herras

ℰℰℰ

*God is greater than the totality of your needs and the human race needs joint together till the end of time.* In God's economy there's no recession. His economic supply sustains the universe and mankind is inexhaustible. Nothing *can deplete God's resources!* God's provisions are available and accessible to everyone who calls upon Him and recognize who He is. His provisions are limitless!

*God is greater than any sickness and diseases.* "By his wounds we are healed" (Isaiah 53:5 NKJV) more than two thousand years ago. You must believe it and received it. God is greater than retina dystrophy or any eye complicated generative disease, not only he can heal it but more so he can create or recreate a new eyeball perfectly free of disease.

God is greater so you should not fear because he is your Father who holds your life, your past, presence and future.

*God is greater than any power on earth, under the earth and in heaven!* He is the absolute power to recognize. Everything is under His authority. There is no darkness or satanic forces that are not subjected to God's power and authority. God is the absolute power and authority in the universe!

## A.  Crucified with Christ

*"I have been crucified with Christ. It is no longer I who live, but Christ who lives in me. And the life I now live in the flesh I live by faith in the Son of God, who love and gave himself for me" (Galatians 1:20 NIV)*

107

### *"I have been crucified with Christ."*

The apostle Paul in the book of Galatians teaches his central message to the churches in Galatia the modern Turkey today. His message was profound and yet simple - *a person is not justified by works of the law but through faith in Jesus* (Galatians 1:16 NIV). One is not justified to salvation by keeping the requirements of the law because the Author of the Law and the fulfillment of the Law is Jesus Christ. Trusting in Christ, believing and receiving Him as Lord and Savior means fulfilling the requirements of the Law which was impossible for humanity to fulfill. There are no good works and human efforts, doctrines and ideologies that can wash, erased and justified one's sin but only in and through the death of Jesus the Lamb of God that takes away the sins of the world.

೭.೭.೭

## "A person is not justified by works of the law but through faith in Jesus."

**Francis Herras**

೭.೭.೭

In Christ one is justified not because he is good, done great in life, keep the requirements of the Law but one is declared not guilty because of the suffering, death and resurrection of Jesus! In Christ a person is washed and justified from sins by virtue of his faith. A person is made holy through the atoning death of Jesus on the cross. Jesus poured out his life and blood to redeem those who repented of their sins, received, accept Jesus as Lord and Savior of their life. Embracing Christ means forgiveness of your sins past, present and future. Embracing Christ means salvation of your soul from the power of sins, death and eternal damnation. You are spiritually made whole (not perfect) by embracing and believing Christ; you are made a new creation. If anyone is in Christ, he is a new creation! Your old sinful life is replaced with Jesus' life in you.

So when the apostle Paul said *"I have been crucified with Christ"* (Galatians 2:20 NKJV) I believe he was referring to his *old lifestyle* crucified with Jesus on the cross. The "I" here is referring to the old self or Paul's old sinful nature that Jesus redeemed on the cross. Paul died with Christ and the life he now lives is the life of Jesus. Christ is now at the center of Paul's life and the motivation of everything he does. The new Paul now shines Christ and advance Jesus kerygmatic agenda in this fallen, lost world that desperately need a Savior and Deliver!

What a great reminder and truth to ponder *"I have been crucified with Christ!"* (Galatians 2:20 NKJV) The old "I" has died with Christ. The sinful "I" died with Christ. The old "I" life style died with Christ. The earthly life style and shallow motivation and agenda died with Christ to advance his kingdom agenda on earth. This means my will your will must be totally aligned and submitted to Christ will. My priorities and your priorities in life change because we've embraced Jesus as Savior, Healer, Sanctifier and coming King. *It implies your earthly perspective was replaced by heavenly perspectives generated from the Word of God. Meaning you've transitioned from self-centered lifestyle to Christ-centered lifestyle;* from self-will to His will; from self-priority to His kingdom priority; from receiving to giving and from existing to living out His original intent and purpose he made you. In other words, your life now is driven by his original design. You no longer live for yourself alone but Christ lives in you; *Jesus now becomes the center of your being - everything revolves around him!* You now live his life in you. You are a *new creation* in Christ!

## B.  You are Made the Righteousness of God

> "God made him (Jesus Christ) who had no sin to be sin for us, so that <u>in him</u> we might *become the righteousness of God*." (2 Corinthians 5:1 NIV)

> "This righteousness is *given* <u>through faith in Jesus Christ</u> to all who believe. There is no difference between Jew and Gentile." (Romans 3:22 NIV)

The righteousness of God was given or imputed "through faith in Jesus Christ" to those who believe Him as their Lord and Savior. Righteousness is given only in Christ and through Christ. *Christians are **made** righteous*

109

*they are not born righteous.* As a child of God, you are MADE righteous by the virtue of your sincere faith in the redemptive work of Jesus. Jesus Christ is the only one that can impute God's righteousness to those who believed Him. Faith in Christ is an essential part of this divine transaction of making believers the righteousness of God.

❧❧❧

# "Christians are made righteous they are not born righteous."

### Francis Herras

❧❧❧

Through faith in Jesus Christ God's righteousness is imputed in you which MADE you the righteousness of God. Positionally in God's eye, you are no longer a lawbreaker because of your faith in Jesus who fulfills completed the requirements of the law - death. In Christ you are made alive! His righteousness made you alive in spirit. His righteousness gives you life eternal. His shedding of the blood on the cross washed away your sins past, present and future thus you become His own child.

God's righteousness was imputed in us through Christ so that you and I can live a new righteous lifestyle by faith in Christ Jesus not for the purpose of salvation but because you are saved and made righteous through faith. This means your good works are the product of God's righteousness that dwells in you.

Since you are made the righteousness of God by virtue of your faith in Christ, safe to confess and declare before God and His people— *"I am the righteousness of God in Christ!"* Go ahead and say it aloud sincerely.

## C. Benefits of God's Righteousness

Let's look at some essential benefits of God's righteousness in your life:

## 1. Peace with God!

Because you are made righteous, justified in Christ and declared not guilty but forgiven and accepted into God's family, you now reconcile with God and at peace with God and in the position to embrace and experienced His peace!

Positionally you have peace with God, meaning, God the Father doesn't see you as hostile, sinner, lawbreaker but He sees Jesus in you the righteousness of God that imputes that righteousness in you that made you the righteousness of God. In other words, God sees you as righteousness not a sinner by virtue of your faith in Jesus. **You now have peace with God!**

"Therefore, having been justified by faith, *we have peace with God* through our Lord Jesus Christ" (Romans 5:1 NKJV).

## 2. You Have Access into His Grace!

> "Through whom also we have access by faith into this grace in which we stand, and rejoice in hope of the glory of God" (Romans 5:2 NKJV).

## 3. Inner Transformation!

> "And not only *that,* but we also glory in tribulations, knowing that tribulation produces perseverance; and perseverance, character; and character, hope" (Romans 5:3-4 NKJV).

## 4. God's Love has been poured out into your Heart!

> "But God demonstrates his own love for us in this: While we were still sinners, Christ died for me" (Romans 5:8 NIV).

God's divine love is in you to enable you love God, yourself and others! It is not man's love but God's divine love in you to forgive others and to love people as God loves them.

## 5. Save from God's Wrath!

> "Since we have now been justified by his blood, how much more shall we be saved from God's wrath through him" (Romans 5:9 NIV).

This means you're saved from eternal punishment—eternal separation from God's presence.

## 6. Reconciled to God!

> "For if, while we were God's enemies, we were reconciled to him through the death of his Son, how much more, having been reconciled, shall we be saved through his life! Not only is this so, but we also boast in God through our Lord Jesus Christ, through whom we have now received reconciliation" (Romans 5:10-11 NIV).

You are reconciled with God. You have a restored relationship with God. You belong into the family of God.

## UPWARD MOMENTUM ACTION STEPS

*Write your answers on a clean sheet of paper.*

In your own words, how will you describe God's greatness?

What is the author saying when he said, "the view from the top?" Was he referring to a literal panoramic view?

How did Moses response to God's view?

What was Paul's central message to the churches in Galatia and how one is justified from sins? Explain.

How do you intend to apply in your daily life, "I have been crucified with Christ. It is no longer I who live, but Christ who lives in me. And the life I now live in the flesh I live by faith in the Son of God, who love and gave himself for me" (Galatians 1:20 NKJV)

How do see yourself as the righteousness of God in Christ?

# CHAPTER 10

# Humility Proclaims "It is Well with My Soul"

*"To be able to say "it is well with my soul" is a humble realization and discovery of true meaning and purpose of suffering, a great loss that the winter of life brings."*
*- Francis Herras*

Many times we don't try to understand and appreciate difficult times or trying seasons of our lives. In winter we focus to see the thick snow, blizzard and the brutal windshield that it brings but not taking quality time to appreciate and ponder the splendor of winter and what does it mean to us as individuals, what it does to the environment, agriculture and economy.

We can think of winter as *"the winter of life"* and see it differently if we only take time to ponder and allow it to speak to us to shape us, transform us, and grow us so we become a person internally changed and transformed by the difficult seasons of life into a better, stronger, and wiser person because we've learned not to resist but think well, not to complain but competent, not to wish for an easier life but becoming a better stronger person.

*Life is difficult.* We lived in a fallen world with morally depraved people. The truth is, we don't naturally say "it is well with my soul" when going through tough season of our lives.

*"It is well with my soul"* is not the natural tendency statement to say

of one in pain and suffering. To be able to say "it is well with my soul" in the midst of seemingly turmoil or grinding moments of life requires time for processing, reflecting, analyzing, questioning, reasoning, and complaining.

To be able to say "it is well with my soul" is to be able to understand the impact of the winters of life, the difficulties that life brings, the various uncertainties and lost opportunities, the many losses of life in many forms, the inner struggles—mentally, emotionally and spiritually.

**⚘⚘⚘**

**"To be able to say "it is well with my soul" is to be able to understand the impact of the winters of life, the difficulties that life brings, the various uncertainties and lost opportunities, the many losses of life in many forms, the inner struggles— mentally, emotionally and spiritually."**

**Francis Herras**

**⚘⚘⚘**

To be able to say "it is well with my soul" is to be able to move forward and painfully overcome any forms of moral, ethical and belief tension roaring inside of you a wave breaking you into pieces in every areas of your life. Parallel to the literal winter, the winters of life has no respecter of person. Everyone goes through it with regularity. Winter come every single year without notice or warning. Winter season has been set. It will come and it will happen according to its design and purpose. You can't control winter. You have no ability to control the seasons. But, you can control and *prepare* yourself for winter so that when it comes you are mentally, physically, spiritually and resourcefully ready to face it. Difficulties, challenges, pain and suffering is a winter of life. They will come and will happen without notice and warning. When it comes, you have two choices to make; one is to RESIST IT and two to REFLECT on

Resist
Reflect
Discover

it and try to DISCOVER its purpose and meaning in relation with your life. Your choice of response to the winter of life will make you or break you; move you forward or hold you back, reform and transform you into a better and wiser person or wreck you into a miserable, depressed person. *Your response to the winter of life determines your outcome.* Winter of life can either pull away from God or push you closer to God depending on how you see it, interpret it and respond to it.

*So saying "it is well with my soul" is not that simple or as a form of opting out yourself from difficulties or totally ignoring the reality of suffering and the pain that it brings in every level of our being, but an acknowledgement of a heart and a mind humbled, shaped, molded, broken, wounded, suffered a loss (in many forms), and most importantly a statement of an examined life.*

You see, to be able to say "it is well with my soul" is a humble realization and discovery of true meaning and purpose of suffering, the great loss that the winter of life brings. One cannot honestly say "it is well with my soul" without authentic understanding the reason behind the winter of life. The only way to discover its meaning and purpose is to go through it and then reflects on what have you become and name its benefits no matter how you are deeply broken, wounded, and struggles and then and only then you will be able to say prayerfully "it is well with my soul."

"It is well with my soul" is a loaded statement coming from the inner sanctum of a person that has gone through challenging winters of life.

"It is well with my soul," is a statement that comes from a heart that appreciates the splendor of the thorns of life and a mindset that embrace the benefits of suffering.

♪♪♪

> ## "It is well with my soul," is a statement that comes from a heart that appreciates the splendor of the thorns of life and a mindset that embrace the benefits of suffering.
>
> **Francis Herras**

♪♪♪

A perfect example is the suffering of our Lord Jesus Christ. His is the ultimate definition of suffering and pain yet it redeems the people of the world from the power of sin, death and hell. Jesus went through the most painful suffering experience. Jesus experienced separation from his heavenly Father when he said "why have you forsaken me?" Jesus experienced separation from his earthly family, and ultimately, loss of his life in a very inhumane form of suffering. *Jesus knew what pain and suffering is and its true meaning and purpose.* He showed us through his suffering, death, and crucifixion. *He knew the reason behind his suffering.* He did not fight neither resist it but he allows it to happen. He went through it because he knew the benefits of his suffering and death bring forgiveness, healing, salvation, and eternal life to those who believe in him. Jesus clearly unfolds to us the real meaning and purpose of his suffering and death. Honestly, not a very positive thing to focus upon given the gravity and level of his suffering yet extremely important that we see as Christian the glory of Christ brutal suffering caused by the very people he came to redeem!

❧❧❧

## "Jesus knew what pain and suffering is and its true meaning and purpose. He knew the reason behind his suffering."

### Francis Herras

❧❧❧

So saying "it is well with my soul" is literally saying what Jesus said to the Father, "nevertheless not my will but your will be done." It was the Father's will for Jesus to suffer and he embraced it. As a Christian, we don't naturally embrace suffering as our Lord Jesus did we resist any forms of suffering on every level let alone to ponder to learn from it and discover its design and purpose. *Yet saying "it is well with my soul" is the best view from the top.* Jesus, saying "nevertheless not my will but your will be done" is the greatest panoramic view from the top one can ever say; total surrender to the will of God in any circumstance no matter how painful, is the

117

perfect view from the top. As a matter of fact a view that Jesus Christ fully embraced. *Jesus showed us the mindset of his kingdom—total submission and surrender to the will of our heavenly Father.*

You see life is not easy. Life in itself is difficult. Life is full of uncertainties and challenging surprises. The only way out is to face those challenges and difficulties and allow them to shape you, changed you, and transformed you into the person God wants you to become.

꧁꧂

## "Jesus showed us the mindset of his kingdom—total submission and surrender to the will of our heavenly Father."

### Francis Herras

꧁꧂

As I look deep in my personal difficult setting or winter of life, I realized the *benefits* that it brings.

- Tremendous growth spiritually, emotionally and mentally; painful sacrifice has strengthens my inner fortitude.
- Tremendous professional growth being a chaplain—providing care services to people with varying degree of health and emotional needs.
- Opportunity to write materials and messages for residents and be able to turn it into a book what you are reading.
- It brings me intimately closer with God in many ways—in prayer, the reading of his words, total dependence and trust in his provisions
- Deepening my patience—driving back and forth for 5 hours from work to home on a weekly basis.
- The 5 hours drive provides me time to educate myself by listening to audio books, do deep thinking, earnest praying and worshipping, as well as planning while driving.

- Opportunity to teach 120 nursing students at Lethbridge College
- Give me plenty of time to know myself better and name growth areas in my life in my current setting.

So, I say, "it is well with my soul" because I know I am doing God's will in my current life's setting.

## A. Identity and Perception

## Psalm 139

How important is Identity?

Identity is undoubtedly an important part of your being. You were given a name by your parents as your identity from the rest of your household that given name has become your social identity whether you love your name or not. *Your personal name is a part of your entire being.* Your family calls you by your name. People at work call you by your name. Wherever you go you introduce yourself to others with your name. You use your name to show who you are when you fill up important government documents such as your passport, your S.I.N., or applying for a job.

## B. Your Name Encapsulates Who You Are

*Your name encapsulates who you are.* You are the epitome of your name. Your name evokes your personality. When people remember you or think of you they remember your attitudes. Everything revolves around your name. People remember your name but they remember who you are because your name and who you are is the same. Your name is an essential identifier of who you are so extremely crucial to look deeply what encapsulates in your name but most importantly the bearer of the name. Meaning to know you better and keep on learning yourself for personal growth and development. The more you know yourself the more you will understand people around you or people working with you or you're working. Aim to know yourself first before making it your goal to know others. Know yourself first to know others better.

உ.உ.உ

# "Your name encapsulates who you are."

### Francis Herras

உ.உ.உ

So here is the first fundamental of moving forward into any relationships, may it be in marriage, family, work, business or ministry.

## C. Know Yourself First

*Your search begins in knowing yourself first.* The starting point in building relationships is not to research other people but to research deeply and honestly yourself. This is hard work in itself. It will need focus and discipline to dig deep and expose the condition of your spirit, soul and mind or your whole being on the operating table of change and personal development.

*You are made to grow, improve and develop by design.* So where do you begin? They're so many things you can do in your beginning point but I recommend that begin with your *identity*.

"How do I see myself?" "What is my personal perception of myself?" Why is this important? It is important because the way you see yourself will affect or impact the way you see or will see other people within your sphere of influence, at home, work or church.

உ.உ.உ

# "You are made to grow, improve and develop by design."

### Francis Herras

உ.உ.உ

Your personal perspective and perception of who you are will affect or impact your perspective and perception of others regardless of cultural, geographical location. Why is this? Because wherever you are there you are. You carry yourself with you including your worldview of yourself.

Let me explain further in the diagram I made for you:

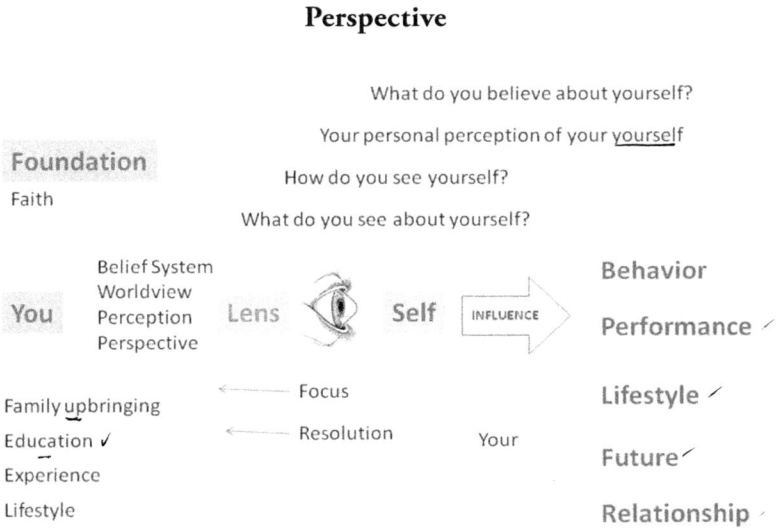

## Perspective

What do you believe about yourself?

Your personal perception of your yourself

**Foundation**

Faith

How do you see yourself?

What do you see about yourself?

| | | | | | | |
|---|---|---|---|---|---|---|
| | Belief System | | | | | **Behavior** |
| | Worldview | | | | | |
| **You** | Perception | Lens | | Self | INFLUENCE | **Performance** |
| | Perspective | | | | | |

Family upbringing  ←——— Focus  **Lifestyle**

Education ✓  ←——— Resolution  Your  **Future**

Experience

Lifestyle  **Relationship**

The only person who can change the focus of your lens is you by focusing it inside of you to the highest resolution possible so you can have a better look inside of who you are. Change the focus of your lens means revisiting and assessing your *belief system* or *worldview* doing necessary correction and refinement to align your life conducive to the God's Word. *Seeing who you are according to God's Word is seeing the way Jesus sees you. Seeing the way Jesus sees you be the best view you can ever have.* Embracing *God's view* of who you are is the perfect view you must see to move forward in life. *Seeing how Jesus sees you is your view from the top your upward momentum.*

**.•.•.•**

## "Seeing who you are according to God's Word is seeing the way Jesus sees you. Seeing the way Jesus sees you be the best view you can ever have."

**Francis Herras**

**.•.•.•**

Develop a healthier positive perspective of yourself so you can relate better with other people. Change yourself from within first. By doing so, you will literally influencing your environment and the surrounding people how they will treat and perceive you.

The response you receive from other people (environment) is connected to your personal perception and perspective of yourself; the way you present yourself, so you have attracted the equivalent result of your own perspective. *It's you creating the impact and results coming from your own perception of yourself. Your perception and perspective of yourself has become the seed sown in your own mind that produces the impact and results in your life.*

**.•.•.•**

## "Your perception and perspective of yourself has become the seed sown in your own mind that produces the impact and results in your life."

**Francis Herras**

**.•.•.•**

The danger is your negative perception of others will attract a negative impact to yourself; those negative perceptions will not help build, improve or grow relationships in any given context. So, extremely important to develop and create a *godly perspective of yourself and a belief that honors God.*

Here are questions for you to think. Please get a piece of paper and a pen to write your honest answers to the following questions:

- Describe your understanding of your own belief? And why?
- What will it make for you to create and develop your own personal perspective of yourself?
- Do you think it will change your life when you develop a belief that honors God?
- In what ways do you think embracing positive mindsets can influence your lifestyle, relationships and professional work?
- Do you think your own perspective has the power to influence and affect your behavior, performance, lifestyle, relationship, business and future?

**Here are general possible outcomes when you have a healthy perspective of yourself:**

- Personal growth
- Confident person
- Happier person
- Higher productivity at work
- Healthier home and relationship
- Positive view of your company
- Increase Retention at work
- Integrity
- Business development
- Positive self-esteem
- Positive perspective
- Positive thoughts
- Positive action
- Positive outcomes

Let me ask you again. *How import is your identity?* Do you agree your identity is significantly important part of your being and daily living? *Aim to know yourself first before making it your goal to know others.* So here is the first fundamental of moving forward into any relationships, may it be in marriage, family, work, business: know yourself first!

Illustration 1: ***What do you see?***

Do you see a glass half full or do you see a half empty glass? Or do you see both? Will *your perspective* affect your behavior and feelings? In what ways do you think your perspective will *affect* you? Do you think your perspective speaks who you are?

Illustration 2: ***What do you see?***

Do you see cloudy day or do you see a sunny day? Or do you see both? In what way do you think *your perspective* of the weather will impact your *feelings*, *attitudes* and *behaviors* if you are a businessperson or a salesperson? Can you name *possible responses* coming from both perspectives?

Your *perception and perspective* has become the seed sown in your conscious and Sub-conscious mind produces results in your life, business, environment and your current reality.

Illustration 3: **What do you see?**

Do you see a green apple? Do you seeds? Do you see apple trees? Do you see fruit bearing apple trees?

The truth is the fruit bearing apple trees are *trapped* inside the green apple unless the *seeds* are planted into the soil those trees won't come out.

Illustration 4: ***What do you see?***

Do you see beautiful roses or thorns or do you see both? Do you see failure and success? Do you see opportunities and difficulties? *What* do you see about yourself? Why is this important to identify and describe them? Because what you see about yourself will influence your feelings, behaviors, performance, relationships and the way you see others.

Here is another example down the point that I am trying to communicate in relation to *the power of your perspective and perception and its influence in so many levels of your being.*

The example I'm giving you was the actual conversation (needs assessment interview) over the phone with a financial advisor struggling to get more clients. Please listen closely to his perspective on the market, interest rate, job, and his business. We'll call him Joe.

**Synopsis of Telephone Interview Needs Assessment Conversation**

> ***Me***: Hi Joe. How are you today? My name is Francis Herras, thank you for taking my call!

Joe, the reason why I am calling is to let you know that we do care of you and your business as financial advisor. We are passionate to see you grow as a person and to see your business succeed.

*Joe*: Oh, I appreciate that thank you.

*Me*: Because we care, our company created Professional Care Development Services to help advisors. I will be working with you directly as your business counselor to guide you in your journey to personal growth and business development. Joe, I have a couple of questions for you to help our company serve you better. Do you have 5 minutes?

*Joe*: Sure.

*Me*: Here is my first question:

What are your *greatest needs* as financial advisor?

*Joe*: "Market is down. Interest rate is low. It's hard to find clients. Lots of employees are laid off from their job."

*Me*: "Joe, is it the economic condition or is it you projecting your perspective and perception of the economic environment? The truth is, you can't control the economic hurdles, interest rate and unemployment influx. But you have full control of how you wish to see or interpret your experience or reality."

*Me*: What somewhat *challenges* are you facing as financial advisor?

*Joe*: "Business is slow. I don't know what to do. I'm nervous. I'm not confident enough. It's hard to look for clients."

***Me***: Joe, the real challenge is your negative perception of the market will not help improve your clientele base and your financial goals. Your perception of the market has limited you to move forward to grow yourself, clients and financial portfolio. I think the real problem is not the market it's how you see the market and interpret things pulling you back to move forward and succeed.

Joe was intently silent for a moment then answered, "no one has ever talked to me the way you do. I've never seen it that way." Joe was happy and was so motivated after our conversation. The following week Joe was present in the Personal Development Training done every Tuesday evening.

Then I close my conversation with Joe by explaining what Professional Care Development Services is.

Joe …

The *Philosophy* behind Professional Care Development Services is Grow yourself to grow your business!

The *Purpose* is to offer you sound coaching and counseling to equip you with Essential Elements needed to your Success and Development.

You remember what Napoleon Hill said, "Definiteness of purpose is the starting point of all achievements."

"All individual achievement begins with adoption of definite major purpose and a specific plan for its attainment. Without a purpose and a plan, people drift aimlessly through life." (Napoleon Hill, Think and Grow Rich)

There are two areas of development we want to guide you succeed:

**1.** Your Personal Development

**2.** Your Business Development Plan

The company will help you in developing tasks and processes generally aiming at developing and implementing growth opportunities in your business; offer you support and monitoring needed implementing those growth opportunities; help you clarify and understand where you are at now in terms of dreams, goals, beliefs and practices essential to personal growth and business development.

Joe, our company care enough to see you grow and succeed!

Will you be interested to come at the office for a 30—45 minutes free consultation and further assessment as a company's care service towards your success?

***Joe***: Sure.

Here is my point, *our perception influence our behavior and performance.* John Maxwell said, "We do not see things as they are we see things as we are." A negative person sees negatively in a positive environment. A positive person sees positively in a negative setting. The fact of matter is we see things as we are not as they are. The *meaning and interpretation* we draw from our reality is pivotal to our performance in accomplishing our target goals. They influence our *feelings* which ultimately impact our *behavior* then our *outcomes.*

ʬʬʬ

# "We do not see things as they are we see things as we are."

## John Maxwell

ʬʬʬ

---

**UPWARD MOMENTUM ACTION STEPS**

*Write your answers on a clean sheet of paper.*

Why is life difficult and full of challenges? Explain.

What does it mean to say "It is well with my soul" in your current reality?

How important is your identity and perception and why?

In what ways your personal perspectives influence your perception of others?

What do you see about yourself? Describe.

---

# SECTION THREE

# THE BENEFITS
# - SUCCESS

# CHAPTER 1

# Humility Capture the
# View from the Top

## A. La Cassa Resort in Kelowna British Columbia

In 2015 of July before embarking on my new work in a financial company as business counselor my family went for a week family vacation at La Cassa Resort in Kelowna British Columbia. La Cassa Resort is amazingly gorgeous place to stay. In my opinion La Cassa is the little Maui version in Canada. My family was captivated by its panoramic scene beyond description. We loved that place.

It was 7 hours to drive from Calgary then we check in get enough rest. Late in the afternoon, my brother-in-law Larry invited us to come over his cottage for coffee. So we went.

The overlooking panoramic view from my cottage was amazingly awestruck and breathes taking experience for us. The smell of clean and fresh air and the soothing sounds of chirping birds I was soaking in and taking everything in, in-printing in my mind the awesome view of the Okanagan Lake right before me. The calm lake back drop with a glorious mountain; the boats and the people water skiing and having fun was captivating and relaxing experienced to me. I thought to myself, indeed there's more to life than work and attending to the daily chores and demands of life—soaking in and allowing nature's glory, serenity, calmness and the fresh, soothing air coming from the Okanagan Lake refreshed my wandering mind and weary body was indeed experiencing life. *So many* times we recognize life but forget to enjoy and experience life itself. We've focused so much to make a living. We have forgotten to make a lifestyle. Even at this very moment I am writing looking at the quiet and serene water of Okanagan Lake is mentally and spiritually nourishing. In deed the glory of nature reflects the God of the universe who created everything. My soul was overwhelmingly praising God for His greatness, wisdom and power displayed in nature.

♪♪♪

## "So many times we recognize life but forget to enjoy and experience life itself. We've focused so much to make a living. We have forgotten to make a lifestyle."

**Francis Herras**

♪♪♪

So my family went for a coffee to visit with my brother-in-law Larry. Little did I know his cottage was located on a *higher elevation?* It took me 5 minutes to drive going to his cottage. His location was right on the top of the mountain. The moment I enter his cottage I went straight to the deck overlooking the Okanagan Lake. *To my surprise, the view from the top was so glorious!* The view from the top was way different from my view at the valley although both are amazing and both locations were positioned in a unique spot. But, *his view from the top has given me a wider panoramic perspective of the entire resort and Okanagan Lake. The view from the top has given me a wider perspective of the same lake from a higher elevation. In other words, change of location has influenced my perspective.*

In this case, the choice of location can hand you wider scope panoramic perspective. It gives me a unique picture of the same lake different from my view in the valley. It was obvious the view from the top has given me a bigger picture of the entire La Casa Resort and the Okanogan Lake comparing it from the view on the valley.

*In just 5 minutes drive my panoramic perspective was change drastically.*

Suddenly I had a better appreciation and understanding of La Casa Resort because of the view I saw from the top. The perspective from a higher elevation was uniquely different from the view from the valley. *The higher elevation scenario has given me a glorious and breathes- taking view and experienced beyond description.*

So I thought to myself I wonder if this *way of thinking* and observation can be applied to belief, money and life style. Meaning, to adopt a wider perspective of life teaching our mind not only to live but experience life, not only to make a living but to make a lifestyle we want.

So let me ask you these questions. Is having more money, a wider income opportunity; more wealth change one's perspective of life? Is being rich, having more money creates wider opportunities to enjoy life by traveling to places so you become the person you want to be? *Is it possible to transition from your present view to the view from the top?* Can you embrace the view from the top without losing the view from the valley?

*I discovered in this short experienced I had that change of location will change your perspective.* In application, it could mean change of career, business, priorities, philosophies or geographical location. So how is your current perspective affecting your lifestyle? In what ways are they influencing your being? Is there a need for you to see your life afresh? Embrace the view from the top.

## B. Perspective will Change you

*Perspective will change your view of thinking.* My five minutes drive from my cottage to my brother-in-law's cottage took me to a higher elevation creates a life changing view from the top experience!

Can we apply this in our personal financial goal planning?

# The View from the Top

# The higher elevation I go the wider perspective

# I see!

# Perspective

The View from the Top

The distance from 53% to 9% is a matter of changing your Perspective!

*2, 5, 10, 15 years*

9%   *SUCCESS*

*FINANCIAL FREEDOM*

53%

Perspective will change you from the inside.

Is it possible to transition from your present view to the view from the top?

14%

24%

The 9 percent on the top of the triangle represent the 9 percent Canadian that are financially secure. Meaning this group of people doesn't have to worry money and their future. The 9 percent have learned the secret of growing their money to work for them. This group had more financial resources than the 90 percent, may be engaged in wider opportunities to make more and acquainted with people of influence in the society. *This 9 percent see things differently.* Not only they work hard and smart but they put their money work hard for them too. They have learned to embrace both view from the valley and the view from the top. They've worked hard for the money but they likewise invest their money work hard for them so that someday when they retire they will have enough to sustain them. They make a living but they further make a lifestyle.

♪♪♪

# "Perspective will change your view of thinking."

**Francis Herras**

♪♪♪

The 53 percent represent Canadians that will still be working at age 65 not because they wanted but because they must because money will not be enough to meet their financial retirement needs. This group of people has money but not enough to sustain them so they are forced to work even at retirement age. If you want proof of this visit Wall Mart, Home Depot or Lowes to interview a couple of them.

Another 14 percent of Canadians are financially broke. They didn't use their credit cards prudently but spend money they don't have on things they don't need. As a result, it put them in a financially difficult condition such as bankruptcy.

At least 24 to 25 percent will be dead at 65. Death is inevitable it comes without warning. The question is will your family continue to live a life they now have when you die? What is your legacy for your loved one's in terms of finances so they can live a decent lifestyle and take care of financial obligations? Do you have insurance coverage needed to protect yourself and your loved ones in the event the inevitable come? Have you thought of that? I can help you.

Furthermore, these statistics shows individual choices. The choice is totally up to you how you view your life, health, finances and your future.

Where do you see yourself in the triangle five or ten years from now? Do you see yourself on the top of the triangle—the 9 percent financially secure Canadians? For me this idea is a view from the top in terms of finances. Personally I want to see myself on the top 10% category someday!

Let's see what God has to say on blessings in His Word—the Bible.

"For I know the plans I have for you," declares the LORD, "plans to *prosper* you and not to harm you, plans to give you *hope* and a *future*" (Jeremiah 29:13 NIV, emphasis mine).

God has *plans* for you. His *plans* are for your ultimate good. Notice the word "plans." That means if you fail He's got another plans for you to succeed. This is God's heart for you and me.

- Plans to *prosper* you
- Plans to give you *hope*
- Plans to give you a *future*

"If you *listen* to these commands of the Lord your God that I am giving you today, and if you *carefully obey* them, the Lord will *make you the head and not the tail,* and you will *always be on top and never at the bottom*" (Deuteronomy 28:13 NIV).

Here is a powerful promise of God to His children signifying their preeminence in terms of economic resources. Listen closely to what He said:

✓ The Lord will *make you the head and not the tail*
✓ You will *always be on top and never at the bottom*

God's promise is for you to be *"the head"* and *"always be on the top"* when you obey His commands. *Meaning when you put Him and His Word first in your life He will fulfill His promise for you.* Is it God's will for you to prosper and succeed in life? Absolutely yes!

Going back with my illustration, the higher elevation I go the wider perspective I see! Elevation change perspective. I realize the perspective from the top not only refreshing and nourishing my soul but more importantly changed me tremendously. The perspective is shaping and making me from inside out. In this short experienced, I've learned that *perspective has the power to change and transformed your mind and ultimately your life when you allow it.*

*God's Word has the power to transform your mind and give you His perspective you needed to succeed and move forward in life. His Word His perspective a view from the top everyone should know!* Let me give two passages of Scriptures that revolutionized my life.

⁎⁎⁎

**"God's Word has the power to transform your mind and give you His perspective you needed to succeed and move forward in life. His Word His perspective a view from the top everyone should know!"**

**Francis Herras**

⁎⁎⁎

## C.  God Gave you the Ability to Produce Wealth

"But remember the LORD your God, for it is he who gives you the *ability* to produce wealth, and so confirms his covenant, which he swore to your ancestors, as it is today." (Deuteronomy 8:18 NIV, emphasis mine) It is God who *"gives you the ability to produce wealth!"* I wonder if this is the mindset rich people embraced. I wonder if they recognize God's given ability to acquire wealth in their success.

One must remember God created human beings and gave them wisdom, understanding, gifts, talents, skills, physical strength and most importantly *health* to acquire wealth. Without those things it will be a challenge to produce wealth.

Remember, the earth is Lord's and everything in it! It is God that gives the rain to water the crops, fruit bearing trees, and gives fertility. Every fishes of the sea, the ox, cattle, sheep, every kinds of animals of the field that produce food for humanity's consumption to live is God's creation. Every fruit bearing fruit trees mango, avocado, guava, star apple, pears, apple, and jackfruit are God's creation that made people become a millionaires.

God owns the mineral resources—the gold, diamond, silver, and various kinds of precious stones and metals that made millions of people around the world become very successful and wealthy. *The millionaires and billionaires of the world must give due credit, honor and glory to God who created the earth resources instrumental to their success.*

Why acknowledge God? Because on Judgment Day rich and poor will stand before God to give an account of their life and the things He entrusted with them on earth. *The glory belongs to God who owns everything!*

Recognizing God who *"gives you the ability to produce wealth"* is your upward momentum. Embracing this view means recognizing God's ownership and sovereignty of everything including your wealth and riches. *For me agreeing with God is a perfect view from the top. Seeing how God sees wealth is a view from the top everyone should know!*

᪥᪥᪥

# "For me agreeing with God is a perfect view from the top. Seeing how God sees wealth is a view from the top everyone should know!"

## Francis Herras

᪥᪥᪥

*Imagine the rich, millionaires and billionaires will give back to God 10 percent of their net income there will be no poverty in the world.* God has provided more than enough for humanity's need it's the greed that is causing the poverty in the world.

Here is another favorite verse.

"Now to *him* who is able *to do immeasurably more than all we ask or imagine*, according to his power that is at work within us, to him be glory in the church and in Christ Jesus throughout all generations, forever and ever! Amen" (Ephesians 3:20-21 NIV, emphasis mine).

*God is "able!" He is able to surpass "what we ask or imagine!"* God is an all-powerful and an all-knowing God who is able to do things beyond human comprehension. He is not limited with our imagination and the things we asked in prayer. God is able to do more for us than we ask, think or imagine!

When God works He works "*immeasurably!*" His thoughts are not our thoughts. His ways are not our ways. God cannot be measured. A God that can be measured ceases to be God. The good news is God only works for the ultimate good of His children especially advancing His Kingdom here on earth.

What have you been asking God lately? What have you been thinking or imagining of your life, family, work, ministry and future? One thing for sure, God is able to do immeasurably more than what you ask or imagine, according to his power that is at work within you!

Look at the slide closely then ask yourself—what probability, possibility, plausibility do I see myself in terms of success, finances or future? What is it that you see yourself doing five or ten years from now? What do you think is the purpose of your existence on planet earth and why?

Probability: The likelihood of something happening, likely to occur

Possibility: A thing that may happen, or be the case

Plausibility: Credible, believable, worthy of approval, appearance of truth
And reason

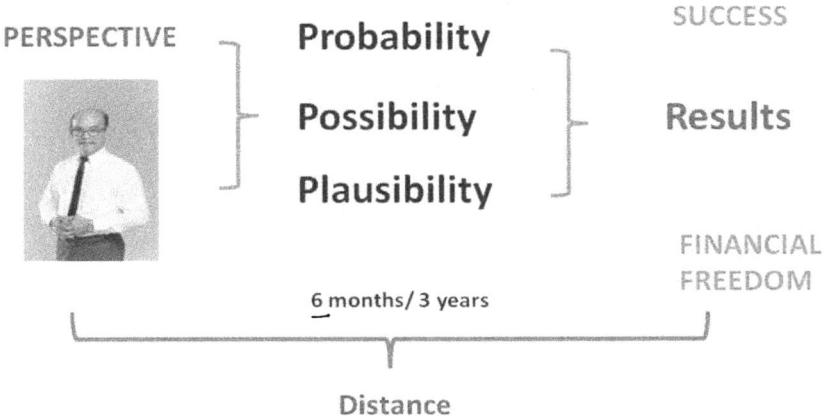

PERSPECTIVE — **Probability** — SUCCESS

**Possibility** **Results**

**Plausibility**

FINANCIAL
FREEDOM

6 months/ 3 years

Distance

## D. The View from the Top and View from the Valley

Let me show you the picture I took overlooking the Okanagan Lake to illustrate the contrast between the view from below and the view from the top to solidify my point is a graphic way.

The higher elevation I go the wider perspective I see!

Elevation change perspective.

## My Point

*The higher elevation I go the wider perspective I see!* Elevation change perspective. I realize the perspective from the top not only refreshed and nourished my soul but more importantly it changed me tremendously from the heart. *The perspective is shaping and making me.* In this short experienced, *I've learned that perspective has the <u>power to change</u> and transformed your mind and ultimately your life when you allow it.*

## Think Again

.ℓ.ℓ.ℓ.

## "I've learned that perspective has the power to change and transformed your mind and ultimately your life when you allow it."

### Francis Herras

.ℓ.ℓ.ℓ.

Perspective has the power to change your life and your future! This means the *distance* from your desired future is a matter of *correcting* your perspective. Meaning you can *transition* from your *'current view'* to the *'view from the top.'* Remember, you are made for the top not the bottom, the head not the tail.

So let me challenge your thinking. I wonder if the perspective being presented can be applied on money and lifestyle. I wonder what riches, wealth and having various streams of income opportunity do in advancing God's Kingdom here on earth.

I wonder how having plenty of money and resources impact the lives of millions around the world as we advance God's Kingdom here on earth. Use them to feed the hungry, providing education to the unprivileged children in remote places, building orphanages in the third world countries, providing health care services facilities for the elderly, funding more mission works on restricted countries. Can you embrace the view from the top?

## E. A Perfect View from the Top

Here is a perfect view from the top.

"Jesus came and told his disciples, "I have been given all authority in heaven and on earth. Therefore, *go* and *make disciples of all the nations, baptizing* them in the name of the Father and the Son and the Holy Spirit. *Teach* these new disciples to obey all the commands I have given you. And be sure of this: *I am with you always*, even to the end of the age." (Matthew 28:18-20 NLT, emphasis mine).

*The Great Commission of Jesus definitely needs large financial resources.* To *go* and *make disciples of all the nations* requires personnel and funding through the church tithes and offerings to fund the Great Commission of Jesus to expand God's Kingdom on earth.

❧❧❧

# "The Great Commission of Jesus definitely needs large financial resources."

**Francis Herras**

❧❧❧

## F. Making the Invisible Visible

God is Spirit. His Kingdom is invisible governed by His principles and will. Holiness, righteousness, peace and justice is the normative mindset of the heavenly kingdom. Worship, fellowship, glory and power are experienced by the saints in His Kingdom. The kingdom of God is the realm where God reigns. The Kingdom of God is where God's will is done and manifested. Our Lord Jesus Christ taught us how to pray in The Lord's Prayer *"Thy kingdom come, Thy will be done in earth, as it is in heaven"* (Matthew 6:10 KJV). This prayer is a powerful prayer desiring to manifest the invisible kingdom of God here on earth through our lives; to make the invisible kingdom visible through the power of the Holy Spirit beginning in our family, sphere of influence, church, community, city, and country. *Jesus lifestyle and mindset have taught us how to manifest God's invisible Kingdom on earth.* His principles and priorities show God's invisible Kingdom. His teachings are kerygmatic in nature. Jesus life oozes the aroma of heaven. His words are medicine to the human spirit, soul and mind. His proclamation of the good news of the Kingdom was the ethos of his entire ministry. Jesus Christ is the perfect example and role model to emulate if we will have to manifest God's invisible Kingdom visible within the realm of our own sphere of influence.

❧❧❧

## "Jesus lifestyle and mindset have taught us how to manifest God's invisible Kingdom on earth."

### Francis Herras

❧❧❧

This is a call to Christians to make the invisible kingdom of God visible through their lives! Your thoughts are invisible. The only way to make them visible is to say it loud to hear and act upon it for people to see and experience. The Word of God is spirit and life, the only way to manifest and make it visible is believed it, live it, say it and experience it. Jesus did not just contain God's Kingdom within himself. He let it shine through his life, teachings, priorities, practices, agendas, and good works. The people in his generation felt the impact, power and influenced of God's invisible Kingdom through Jesus' life and ministry on every level of the known society—politically, socially, religiously and individually!

---

## UPWARD MOMENTION ACTION STEPS

*Write your answers on a clean sheet of paper.*

What is the author saying when he said, "the view from the top?" Was he referring to a literal panoramic view?

How did Moses response to God's view?

What was Paul's central message to the churches in Galatia and how one is justified from sins? Explain.

How do you intend to apply in your daily life, "I have been crucified with Christ. It is no longer I who live, but Christ who lives in me. And the life I now live in the flesh I live by faith in the Son of God, who love and gave himself for me." (Galatians 1:20 ESV)

How you do see yourself as the righteousness of God in Christ?

---

# CHAPTER 2

# Allow Inner Change to Create Outer Change

*"A lowly spirit is demonstrated when one associates with the poor. It is this spirit alone which does not despise any who are created by God. God's presence and glory is manifested in the life of the spiritually humble."*[57]
*Watchman Nee*

"Therefore, I urge you, brothers and sisters, in view of God's mercy, to offer your bodies as a living sacrifice, holy and pleasing to God—this is your true and proper worship. Do not conform to the pattern of this world, but *be transformed by the renewing of your mind.* Then you will be able to test and approve what God's will is—his good, pleasing and perfect will" (Romans 12:1-2 NIV emphasis mine).

Why change? What is the basis of change? What is the purpose of change? Who start change? How do you measure inner change? What happens when you don't change? To whose standard should you pattern change? How do you know you've changed? These are loaded questions I guess but one must answer them honestly for authentic change to happen. Real change happens when you make it happens in partnership with God through the agency of His Words the Bible that has the power to penetrate your inner being.

---

[57] Nee, Watchman. <u>Journeying Towards The Spiritual</u>. New York: Christian Fellowship Publisher, c. 2006. P. 135.

Experientially, change is not that simple. It's easier said than done. It is a difficult and frustrating transformational undertaking to aim. For example, you've set your goals up for the year, forecasted your desired outcomes, yet sticking and disciplining yourself to work it out takes focus, discipline, lots of mental, emotional, physical energy, and consistent strategic prayer planning.

The reason why *change is difficult is that you are basically deconstructing and reconstructing the state of your heart to a higher moral and ethical standard.* You are literally changing your moral compass into a better compass; by doing so, you enter into a realm that is unfamiliar and new to your old pattern of thinking, perception, lifestyle, and belief formation. What you are doing is intentionally breaking away from your old habits, an old mindset, an old practice, old lifestyle, and old perspective reconstructing a new belief worldview and lifestyle as you move forward to your desired future.

♪♪♪

# "The reason why change is difficult is that you are basically deconstructing and reconstructing the state of your heart to a higher moral and ethical standard."

**Francis Herras**

♪♪♪

Inner change will need your whole being for it to happen. Inner change will need your total determination, sincere want and discipline to change for better. *Inner change will need uncompromising focus, total cooperation and total commitment to the picture of change you wish to see in yourself.*

Change happens when you make it happen. Change happens when you *think* change, *talk* change, *desired* change, *commit* to change, *live* a changed life and become an *agent* of change in your sphere of influence.

You can't control your external environment (work, church,

neighborhood, etc.) but *you have the power to make change happen inside of you when you want to change for God's glory!*

The only sensible and meaningful change that will make a huge impact in your life is the change from the heart. *Outer change is a result of inner change. Inner change creates external change.* The agency of external change is the internal change. Change always starts from within you.

Here are examples of change? Change is constant and inevitable.

- ✓ **Organizationally** companies change technology, leadership and personnel to increase efficiency and lower costs.
- ✓ **Management** change to give employees new knowledge, skills, and effective performance for better outcomes.
- ✓ **Professionally** a change of work for a better opportunity, more challenges, and career growth.
- ✓ **Relationally** change for better intimacy, better emotional intelligence, positive communication, growth and personal development in every facet of your human life.
- ✓ **Physiologically** change due to aging. Meaning you're not getting younger but advancing in age. If you don't believe me for the sake of illustration, take an old picture of yourself and your recent picture put them side-by-side to see the change.
- ✓ **Corporately as a business** change for profitability, efficiency, relevancy, influence, growth, development and expansion just to name a few.

There are so many identifiable reasons for change as an individual, as a business, as a family, as a church or as a leader. One thing for sure, change is constant. Change will come. Change will happen. There is no doubt. But, the real bigger issue is literally the reason behind change. In other words, it extremely essential to name the purpose of change and the new meaning change will bring. In short, you don't only make the change to happen but discover the purpose and the meaning of that desired change. The purpose of change must be pronounced for change to birth new meaning. Change for the sake of change doesn't have meaning. But change to carry out God-given purpose is everything. Purpose drive and trigger change. Change in the absence of purpose will have no impact but change to carry out purpose gives meaning.

Purpose triggers change. Change gives meaning. Meaning clarifies identity. Let me illustrate by drawing a diagram.

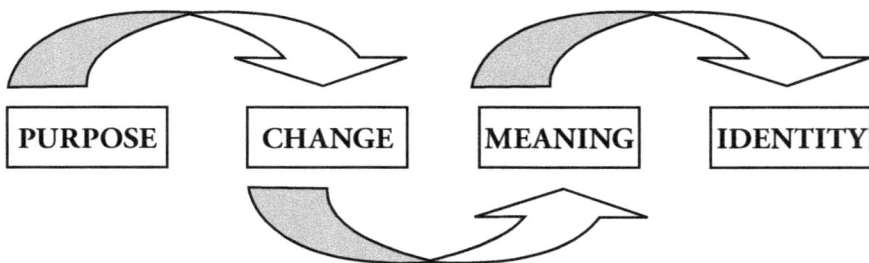

The WHY of change is essential to know for lasting and meaningful results. To put this into perspective, purpose is the most important thing than change itself. Here is why. Change without purpose is meaningless. But change to carry out purpose is a meaningful choice. The point is - not just change but knowing *why* and *what* the change is or will do. So, change is the vehicle of purpose. Purpose is the goal and destiny of change. One must consider these when initiating change personally, corporately, organizationally, relationally. Put in mind change don't happen in a vacuum. You start change according to your God-given purpose and desired outcome of that change. *You're not change by chance you are changed by choice you make in connection to your purpose.*

Change in the neighborhood, is a result of changed in the hearts and minds of the people that lives in the neighborhood. Change at work policy, is a result of a change in the minds of the key leaders (change maker) of the company. Change in the home, is a result of a change in the hearts and minds of the household members beginning from parents.

*Change doesn't just happen in a vacuum, it happens when desired and sought desperately for good cause and reason.* For example, change in relationships, is a direct result of a change in the minds among the parties involved. In other words, outer change in life is a result of one's inner change of heart.

𝓛𝓛𝓛

# "Change doesn't just happen in a vacuum, it happens when desired and sought desperately for good cause and reason."

**Francis Herras**

𝓛𝓛𝓛

*Change is a cause-and-effect.* When you change inside, the result will be a change in your outside environment. People around you will begin to notice your positive change. They'll make a comment such as, "Something is different in you, your thoughts and behavior." In short, *your external environment will positively respond to your internal change.* Your sphere of influence will be drawn and attracted to the positive change happening inside of you. This is the cause and effect of change—you being the first beneficiary, and second, your surroundings.

*Positive change attracts positive things.* Negative change attracts negative things. When you commit to change inside, the forces of good comes to your aid. On the other hand, the forces of evil, comes to your opposition to change. Evil, hate godly changed. Evil, hates moral changed. Evil forces will do every possible thing to pull you away from your goal outcomes. The stronger the evil forces (including the negative people around you) pulls you, is because, darkness is reacting with your newly found changed in Christ.

When you see the painful piercing of darkness is because you are breaking through it. It is because you are breaking through from your old habits, old thinking pattern and old lifestyle and developing a brand new thinking pattern, the mind of Christ. Your focus has changed—upward.

You now begin to see forces of darkness that doesn't prefer to let you go. You need a higher power bigger than yourself to overcome. You need the power and intervention of Jesus in your life. Jesus must become the Lord, Savior and Master of your life to rise above your weakness and limitations. Jesus must be enthroned at the center of your heart. Self and negativity must be dethroned from your heart.

Jesus is your hope for change, future and eternity. When you receive Jesus in your heart as your Lord and Savior, you are headed for a total series of good, yet painful changes in life, because Jesus' life in you will create the necessary change you may not want according to his plan and purpose for your life.

Your eternal destiny will change when Jesus is at the core of your being: your priorities change, habits change, mindset change, perspective change, state of the heart change. Jesus spirit will begin to manifest through you in so many ways. Your surrounding will be influenced by that manifestation. Your environment will react, respond either positively or negatively to the life of Jesus manifesting through you. When you noticed this signs happening, know for sure, real change has come upon you, inner change has come upon you, spiritual regeneration has come upon, and you are now living the kingdom mindset back up with the kingdom life style.

Can we apply what change is in terms of work? Or in what you do?

## A. Making a Living or Designing a Lifestyle?

Here is a question for you to ponder. *Are you making a living or designing a lifestyle?* Just before I answer that question, let me give you what the experts is saying to workforce.

Experts claims that eighty percent (80%) of the workforce today are either misplaced or misfit at workplace. My assumption is potentially happening both in the corporate and non-profit organizations around the world.

.♪.♪.♪.

# "Are you making a living or designing a lifestyle?"

### Francis Herras

.♪.♪.♪.

Imagine going to work every day knowing that 80 percent of your coworkers are either misplaced or misfit from their works? This could mean different things. This could potentially entail many employees not genuinely happy in what they do at work. They work solely to earn a living because they must meet or their family need. There is absolutely nothing wrong with providing financially family needs. *I think the problem lies on the fact that employees are not happy, struggling, misplaced, a misfit in what they do at work place.* Secondly, this could easily translate into frequent turnover, tardiness, sick leave, and waste of companies' resources and who knows what else. Waste of time, energy, talents and skills. Lastly, it could mean employees not pursuing their dreams, their design, their passion, purpose or the things that they wanted to do in life; put aside their desired future because they're stuck on a job that meets their family needs. The bigger challenge with this picture is a huge inner struggle, loneliness, potential relationship conflict at work and at home, feeling unsatisfied and unfulfilled.

The bottom line is personal and professional development is at stake. Vision and dreams be put aside doing something you're not happy until you retire at 65 years old. So let me ask you again, are you making a living or designing a lifestyle that you want to see, love and experience?

This is the reason *why* I am doing what I am doing. This is *why* I am passionate to **help unsatisfied employees build momentum to win in life so they can enjoy their work and meaningful lifestyle.**

This is *why* I've written this book you're reading and Forward Momentum—the Art in Winning in Life to offer a practical guide in the art of winning in life to encourage readers create a forward momentum that will take them to their desired life and future.

So how do you approach this dilemma between making a living and designing a lifestyle? Is there a way to at least to reduce that 80 percent? I don't know the answer because; I am one of that 80 percent. But let me tell you what I know from my personal experience. *Exiting from the 80 percent, being misplaced and misfit means giving up your salary and the benefits that your work provides is not easy to do especially when you have children to raise and bills to pay.*

Here is a loaded question for us workers regardless of the field of work or profession. This question has been asked by the richest person during his days. His name was King Solomon. Listen, what he has to say.

## B. What do I gain from my Current Work?

*"What do workers **gain** from their toil"* (Ecclesiastes 3:9 NIV, emphasis mine). Have you ever asked that question to yourself? If not, why don't you try asking yourself right now, *"What do I gain from my current work?"* Then list your honest answers on a piece of paper on gains in what you do at work. Name the gains you benefited from your current job?

Let's continue listening with Solomon.

"I have seen the burden God has laid on the human race. He has made everything beautiful in its time. He has also set eternity in the human heart; yet no one can fathom what God has done from beginning to end. *I know that there is nothing better for people than to be happy and to do good while they live.* That each of them may *eat and drink*, and **find satisfaction in all their toil**—this is the gift of God." (Ecclesiastes 3:10-13 NIV, emphasis mine).

"So I saw that there is nothing better for a person than to **enjoy their work**, because that is their lot" (Ecclesiastes 3:22 NIV, emphasis mine).

Let's extract Solomon's perspective on work shall we. Solomon's insights of advice to workers/employees are obvious: Be happy, do well while you live. Eat and drink and find satisfaction in your toil (work)—the gift of God. There is nothing better for a person than to enjoy their work because that is their lot (*calling or purpose in life*). This is an advised from a person who has everything and tried everything in search for the meaning of life.

For Solomon, *happiness, doing good and being satisfied in living out your purpose or call* in life (your work) is better than everything else. So what was he trying to tell us? What can we learn from him?

Was Solomon saying to the 21st century workers (employees/professionals) be happy, do well and be satisfied while enjoying your work? If he is, are you happy, do well, satisfied and enjoying your current work? If not, why not? What's the solution? I think the solution to this problem can be found on the answer you personally provided to Solomon's question, **"What do workers gain from their toil?"** (Ecclesiastes 3:9 NIV, emphasis mine). The gains you enumerated earlier. What have you become as individual as an employee or a business owner? Did you find meaning in what you do and become?

Let's look at work and define work if we can through the lens of the Scripture and Wisdom of Solomon. First let's ask, "What is work?"

## C.  What is Work?

Solomon defines work as being a **"*lot*"** a gift from God. He associated work with God's *calling* and *purpose* in life, this was his perspective. *Meaning* **in Solomon's mind** *your work is God's call upon your life to carry out your purpose.* It is through your work (God's call) you carry out your purpose in life. This means you express your life's purpose through your work. So, if work is a call of God to do, then you and I must value and treat our work with dignity. ***So many employees struggle at work not because they don't want to work but somewhat they have not discovered yet their life's purpose of what they do at work.*** In other words, they fulfill God's call to work but have no understanding if work correlates with their purpose in life. *There is a gap between work and purpose.* This gap between work and purpose could potentially lead into *internal distress* that could potentially express itself to various psychosomatic illnesses if not augmented.

᳞᳞᳞

## "Solomon defines work as being a "lot" a gift from God. Meaning work is God's call upon your life to carry out your purpose."

### Francis Herras

᳞᳞᳞

Many of us see the importance of work *not through the lens of God's call* but *'the need to work'* to make a living. *Meaning we work for a paycheck but not to do our purpose.* This is why so many employees and professionals out there working so hard unmotivated, struggling and dissatisfied with what they do.

Happy employees tend to do well in their work. They enjoy their work.

Work increase their level of happiness, it gives them a feeling of satisfaction, purpose and meaning to keep doing well in what they do. While unhappy employees drag themselves to work and look for a reason not to work and expect to get paid. Their level of happiness continues to spiral thus becomes unsatisfied in what they do and ultimately becomes unproductive and a liability to the resources of their company because they were not able to understand the connection between their work and purpose in life.

This leads me to the next question, "why work?"

## D.  Why Work?

Why work? Why do we get up every day to go to work? Here is my simple and practical answer to that question. ***We work to fulfill God's call to work to do our purpose in life.*** Work is more than just monthly pay check cash in every pay day. *We work to carry out our God-given purpose.* By doing so, *our purpose gives us meaning* although work doesn't define us God does, work gives us a sense of purpose of existence. *In other words expressing our God-given purpose through work is indeed the essence of work and quality of humility.*

❧❧❧

# "Expressing our God-given purpose through work is indeed the essence of work and quality of humility."

**Francis Herras**

❧❧❧

God Himself is a great worker indicated in the creation account in the book of Genesis. *Work is God's idea.* The universe is a product of His work. God's work not only reflects His wisdom, power, creativity but likewise His nature and good intent with His creation. *Work is an expression of God's being to his universe so our work should be an expression of our being in our workplace.* God along with the angelic beings celebrated His work of creation then rested on the seventh day according to Genesis chapter 1 and 2. *This Implies that you and I today must work, celebrate our work but take enough time to rest (Sabbath of rest) to recuperate our spirit, soul and body. God did not design us just to work but to work to carry out our purpose of existence here on earth.* When you work for a paycheck you are making a living but when you work to do your purpose, you are designing a quality lifestyle—a lifestyle driven by your purpose in obedience to God's call to work.

ℓℓℓ

## "God did not design us just to work but to work to carry out our purpose of existence here on earth."

### Francis Herras

ℓℓℓ

I think the choice is not between just enough or more than enough money at the end of the month. *I think the choice is between making money for a living or designing a quality lifestyle.* More importantly, the person you are becoming at work. The happiness and the satisfaction facet must be considered doing your work with a good understanding of *what is it that you wanted to do in life through your work* as Solomon calls it, your "lot" a gift of God. Your work is your lot a gift from God. Your work is your zone to do your purpose in life.

As a Christian, do you see your work a form of worship? Is work supposed to be a form of worship?

### E. Is Work supposed to be a form of Worship?

Someone said the highest occupation of man is worship. The Bible tells us **in everything** you do, do it for the glory of God. Is work supposed to give glory to God? *Is work supposed to be a form of worship?* How many employees do you know think goes to work with that mindset? This will drastically revolutionized and change work environment for better!

Just imagine, employees worshipping God through their work at their workplace! Granted that work should be a form of worship to God; personally, I'm not sure if I am worshipping God through my work at my workplace. The truth is, I have attempted to resign from my work. I have forward my resignation letter but was denied. My director wanted to keep me. He wants me to stay to keep doing what I am doing as a chaplain. But honestly, everything inside of me is screaming, look for another job closer to your family where you are happy!

## F. Balancing the Dilemma: Making a Living vs. Making a Lifestyle?

*So how do we find a balance between making a living and making a lifestyle?* In my opinion, the focus should be the *purpose behind making a living and making a lifestyle.* **Purpose** *should neutralize the dilemma. Living should be more than just making money or making a lifestyle but likewise discerning your ultimate purpose in life and living it out through your work.*

In other words, integration of these philosophical perspectives is crucial to your success in life. Instead of making these philosophies compete with each other in mind, *why not integrate, and create one philosophy* that will propel you to happiness, do good and being satisfied in what you do?

Why not say, "I am *making a living* to create my *desired lifestyle* in fulfillment of my ultimate *purpose* in life."

This means making a living while you are living out your purpose. This means creating a lifestyle while living according to your purpose. This means creating a purpose-driven life more than just making a living and making a lifestyle. So the choice is yours—making a living driven life, making a lifestyle, or living a purpose-driven life? *I chose the integration of the three, making a living to create my desired lifestyle in fulfillment of my ultimate purpose in life for the glory of God!*

૱૱૱

# "I chose the integration of the three, making a living to create my desired lifestyle in fulfillment of my ultimate purpose in life for the glory of God!"

**Francis Herras**

૱૱૱

## G. Life is a Mixture of Opportunities and Difficulties

Life is wonderful but hard, full of struggles and difficulties. Success is achievable but not easy. It requires focus, discipline, precise goals and desired outcomes you want in life.

*Life is a mixture of opportunities and difficulties.* Regardless of your current condition, life moves fast. Life is designed to grow and progress in difficult times and in good times. We need both ingredients to succeed. A good illustration are roses and thorns; pain and pleasure; opportunities and difficulties; life and death; death and resurrection. Informed realization and understanding of these are keys to overcome and to move you forward with great momentum.

No one is exempted from the testing and troubles of life. Believers and unbelievers alike will go through the negative and positive experience that life will bring. Just as the sun rises to warm the universe so difficulties and opportunities rises upon church and non-church people. Regardless of your belief, you are not exempted from the laws of the four seasons God had prearranged. Everyone go through winter, spring, summer, and fall. Whatever the four seasons will bring to life, one thing for sure, the four seasons will always come upon the people who love God and the people who don't believe in God.

## H. Set the Sail of your Mind

*The wind blows to everyone so as opportunities and difficulties.* You can't control the four seasons and the blowing of the wind, when and where the wind will blow. The only thing that you can control is the set of your sail figuratively. You can't control difficulties and trying moments that comes into your life, but, you can control the set of the sail of your mind so that challenging moment's push you forward than pulls you downward. Your perspective and understanding of what you think is the design of difficulties is your forward momentum to propel you to your desired outcomes in life.

This morning I was not feeling very positive and enthusiastic due to many things in mind.

One is, a large sum of money needed for the development of my basement due flooding, renewal of mortgage, the possibility of accessing home equity to buy another property closer at work; being away from my family five days a week because of work which entails traveling five hours a week from home to work; being away alone while working plus an added $1200 expense monthly rental, gas, food expenses; my doctorial studies, dissertation, editing my book, and look for a new job in Calgary. These are just a few things that occupied my mind. Deep inside, I felt I absolutely need a respite to refresh myself mentally.

I definitely need a moment of relief. So, what I did to alleviate my lack of enthusiasm was, took my I phone, turn it on my YouTube channel, and then listen to my favorite worship songs. While listening, I started worshipping and praying.

I honestly pour out heart to Jesus. I let him know what I felt and thought. It was a moment of total transparency and intimate moment with my Lord Jesus. After that, I started feeling good. I felt strengthens, heard, loved and comforted driving to work. The short, yet sweet, and honest worship and prayer creates that upward momentum to keep me going.

*We need an upward momentum in so many areas of life, especially during those overwhelming times.* We need a moment that will strengthen, inspire, encourage, focus, and clarity to move forward in spite of the challenges before us. Mine was worship and prayer. What's your? Have you taken time to discover your upward momentum moments to keep you going?

## I.   What is Momentum?

According to Online Etymology Dictionary, it means, *"quantity of motion of a moving body."* Momentum is a Latin word, which means, *"movement, moving power."* [58]

This is what happens to me after a sweet short worship and prayer. I felt a boost of power inside of me that moves me forward which leads me to remind myself and look at myself in front of the mirror— "Francis you are okay, you are a child of God, loved by God and provided by God, you're not alone, and you are safe." After that, I'm ready for work. I felt the movement moving power of Jesus in my spirit. *My upward momentum creates my forward momentum to work.*

---

[58] http://www.etymonline.com/index.php?allowed_in_frame=0&search=momentum

UPWARD MOMENTUM ACTION STEPS

*Write your answers on a clean sheet of paper.*

Are you making a living, designing a lifestyle or
accomplishing your purpose in life?

What do you gain from your current work?

What is work in your own words and why work?

How would you explain life is a mixture of
opportunities and difficulties?

How would you apply set the sail of your mind and
the concept of momentum in your life?

# CHAPTER 3

# Humility Understand the Difference Between Responsibility and Deserving

Here is the big question. Do we deserve to exist? Do we deserve to enjoy the day, sunshine, the moon, the stars, the magnificent mountains, the ocean, animals, birds, fishes of the sea and plants, crops and refreshing good looks of the trees?

Do we deserve to live a quality life? Do we deserve healthy life style? Do we deserve good high paying job? Do we deserve the highest title in our company? Do we deserve healthy relationships with our spouse and children and friends? Do we deserve good things in life? Do we deserve success and a bright future?

How many of you have asked at least one or two of those questions? And what answer did you discover to your question on deserving?

## A. Grade Twelve Student

Let's have a closer look on the word deserve. Does a grade twelve student deserve a good grade in his report card? What do you think is the answer? Not if he did his job. Not if he did his responsibility to study and read the books and meet the paper works requirements and attendance required to have a good grade. That student can't just sit around and do nothing and say, I deserve, I deserve, I deserve a high grade the whole day! That's not going to happen. Good grades are not an entitlement but a product of responsible study, thinking, point of view, behavior and discipline. High grades are responsibility more than entitlement. *You make a good grade to deserve it.*

## B. A Farmer

What if a farmer sit in front of his farm and shouts, I deserve a good, bountiful harvest and do nothing? He speaks to the farm, grow crop grow, I deserve a harvest! It doesn't work that way. First the farmer must *plow* the ground, *plant* the seeds and then *water* the seeds. In the absence of these three responsible acts no bountiful harvest. The farmer plants the seeds then God grow the seeds.

A good harvest is a partnership with the God of the universe. You do your responsibility then God will do his part. As a responsible farmer you do the hard work, and then God gives you the reward for your hard work. *Your hard work brings you success not because you deserved but because you did your part as a responsible steward to do the right thing.* When you do the hard work, the right things, work on priorities, set up your goals one day you reap the fruits of your work. In short, you will succeed. *In this case, you succeed not because you deserved but because you make success happen.* You deserved the fruits of your hard work and success you created. Meaning you fulfill your responsibility to deserved your success in partnership with God.

Here is the thing, don't settle for easy things do the hard work! There is no such thing as easy life. The truth is life has never been easy. Life is difficult. If you don't believe me just visit a delivery room and watch two lives in struggles, the mom giving birth and the baby coming out from warm comfort zone. Life has never been easy so don't be deceived to settle on easy stuff do the hard things, do your responsibility first then reap the harvest of your hard work later.

I mean you don't tell your children, eat the dessert first if you wanted a salad. No, you tell your children, eat the salad first if you want the dessert. Do the hard work first and then you'll get your reward. That is what God does to his children. Do your responsibility first. Do the hard work first. Eat the broccoli first. Eat the green apple a day first then you'll see a result of your health. Do the right things no matter how difficult and hard because reward is coming later, harvest is coming later, success is coming later. Focus on your goals and dreams and be determined to do them.

Be a *good steward* in everything God has provided you. Appreciate the Seasons and be responsible to use each season for your favor. Don't curse the season or the weather or those things that God has provided you to become successful in life but enjoy them and let them work their purpose and design to grow and mature you. Experience the season, learn the season, live the season and use the season to carry out your God-given potentials.

## C. Adam and Eve

Adam and Eve the first couple did not deserve the Garden of Eden, they did not deserve paradise with its treasures, rivers, trees and animals. *God placed them in the Garden he made Himself.* We don't deserve to exist on planet earth but God made the human race exist on earth and make earth the home of the human race he made in his image for a purpose. The couple doesn't deserve the best and the great things in the Garden *God granted and provided* it to them because in God's sovereignty that's the right thing to do to care for them.

God cause the universe and everything in it including man. He is the Cause of everything good in the universe. As a responsible Father of creation he put order in the universe and essential provisions for humanity to multiply, nourished, grow and live. God cared for his creation. *God provided a home for the first couple and family because it was the right thing to do not because they deserve it.*

## D. Israel

Israel was chosen by God not because they deserve as a nation to be chosen by God. The choosing of Israel was God's choice based on his sovereign will. Could he choose other nation other than Israel? Absolutely, He could but he chose Israel. Does God have the right to his choice as the creator and owner of the entire universe? Absolutely he owns everything!

✓ Do you deserve to be here or did God allow you to exist?

✓ Do you deserve to live or did God breathed the breath of life in you in your mother's womb?

✓ Do you deserve to live a healthy life without doing your responsibility eating healthy, proper diet?

✓ Do you deserve promotion at work without performing well and doing your responsibilities and accountabilities?

✓ Do you deserve success without working hard, having the right spirit, relationships and goals?

✓ Do you deserve to receive a salary without being employed to add value in the company you work?

## E.  Good Health

If you wanted to be healthy, you must eat healthy and do healthy activities. Good h*ealth is a result of your choice and doing your responsibility and goals to be healthy.* The truth is, you are responsible for your own health not MacDonald or the Alberta Health Care. The key to your better health is *you* so don't blame Pizza Hut, Wendy's or Crispy Crème, or Tim Horton's. Blame the person in the mirror for not making responsible choices for a better health future. You can't just keep eating a pizza and fries and tell yourself I deserve to be healthy and sit or sleep the whole day without going out for a walk, run and necessary exercise to keep you functionally healthy. *Healthy and health is your responsibility to do to make it happen in your life and your family.*

You are responsible for your own health not the government. They don't buy your groceries and cook your food you do. The government doesn't take you to the fast food restaurant you do so don't blame the government if you're 40, 140 or 240 pounds overweight. You can argue with yourself and think, I'm not overweight by bones are growing heavier; I have big and heavy bones that's the 140 pounds excess. I'm not overweight my bones are getting bigger that's why. It's not fat it's my bones! Stop making excuses and be responsible for your health now for a healthier tomorrow.

You don't deserve to be clothed it's the right thing to do. You don't deserve to take a shower it's the right thing to do. You don't deserve to brush your teeth it's the right thing to do. If you don't they'll take you away into a mental institution.

*Deserve disrobe you of your responsibility to do the right thing.* Deserve disrobe you to do the hard thing, exercise your brilliance, wisdom, creativity, goals, dreams and vision.

*Deserve is a form of entitlement mentality that will disrobe you of doing your responsibility. Deserved is a form of dependent mentality to hand over things you want without working.*

**"Deserve is a form of entitlement mentality that will disrobe you of doing your responsibility. Deserved is a form of dependent mentality to hand over things you want without working."**

**Francis Herras**

### F. The Cause-and-Effect Principle

What do we do? You must understand the principle of cause and effect. Good grades are cause and effect. Good health and success is cause and effect. Good future is cause and effect. Everything is cause and effect.

Understanding the cause-and-effect principle is essential to your success. This means whatever you plant you will reap. When you cause yourself to study hard, finish your desired degree according to your purpose the effect will be a good job in the future if you don't give up the momentum of moving forward and keep on keeping on serving people.

It is cause and effect. It's the principle of sowing and reaping which reflects a responsibility.

When you plant a mango seed, you expect a mango tree and a harvest of mango fruits. This is where the miracles happen. You plant a seed but you harvest more. One seed multiplies. The cause is one seed, and the effect is more fruits which results into more seeds.

The principle of multiplication that God built in the mango seed DNA. What if you didn't plant a mango seed? Will you expect a harvest? What if you didn't save money for your retirement will you have something to live on when you retire?

If you save 10% of your income starting now in ten years, you'll multiply your money. A $10,000 savings with compounded interest rate of 12% per year will accumulate up to $640,000 in twenty years. What if you spent your $10,000 for a vice instead of saving it for your retirement what do you think will happen? You're right there be nothing to accumulate. This means you will arrive in a future you don't want to see. Then what, you start blaming your company, the government, the taxes and your salary. You are responsible for your own retirement not the government not your company you. The key to a better retirement is *you* not the government. The key to your better future is *you* not other people!

## G. The Key to your Better Future is You

Let me share with you great ideas from Jim Rohn that deeply affected my life and influence my thinking positively.

"The key to your better future is you." (Jim Rohn)

> "To be successful, you must work hard on yourself more than you work hard on your job. When you work hard on your job, it gives you money but when you work hard on yourself it gives you a fortune." (Jim Rohn)

> "For things to change in your life you must change." (Jim Rohn)

> "Don't wish things were easier wish you were better. Wish for more wisdom." (Jim Rohn)

The reality is working hard on yourself is not easy. It needs focus and discipline and a constant reminder with yourself in those areas that you are working on in your life. Working hard on yourself calls for humility, pure honesty, a deeper and a closer look into your heart and mind to be able to name key areas of improvements in your quest for quality of life and success. *Truly, the key to your personal success is you in partnership with God.* Why you? Because no one else who understand the way you understand yourself and no one sees you the way you see yourself. Furthermore, it's only you who can honestly show and name key areas of improvements in your life in terms of your goals, ambitions, spirit, and relationships. It is only you who can do this with a strong passion and determination to become better in your Christian life wherever you are.

♪♪♪

# "Truly, the key to your personal success is you in partnership with God."

**Francis Herras**

♪♪♪

Working hard on yourself means setting up a well-defined goals and executing those goals according to priorities. When you don't have goals, you're a train without a track. It will be impossible to move forward to reach destiny the train must have a track to travel.

The train tracts are goals in life to a better future. If you don't have goals, you can start creating right at this very moment. Stop whatever you are doing right now and start working on your goals.

*Defining your goals is the starting point of your success.* Goals are pictures of your desired future remember no goals no picture, no picture no future. Or you might end up in the future you don't want to see because you did not plan your future. Certainly without defined goals you will have to arrive in the future you might regret, frustrated and disappointed; see a lifestyle you don't want, live in a house you don't want, work on a job you hate; drive a car you don't want to drive because you fail to take time to create your goals your guide to your future.

*Setting up goals is hard work but working hard on your goals will take you to your future with precision.* Work on your goals now to create your tomorrow. Seize your future now by designing it through your goals. *Sharpen the focus and resolution of your future by sharpening the focus and resolution of your goals today.*

.℣.℣.℣

# "Sharpen the focus and resolution of your future by sharpening the focus and resolution of your goals today."

**Francis Herras**

.℣.℣.℣

## H.  Building a Solid Financial Foundation for Life

How do you build a solid financial foundation?

✓  **First acknowledge God the Source of your financial provisions!**

God is your ultimate provider by virtue of being your heavenly Father. God knew your present and future needs and knew when you need them. He is always on time in blessings his children. God's provisions will never be depleted regardless of economic recession. God's economy is not subjected to earthly economic principles or procedure. Everything on earth is subjected to God's principles. He's got in his hand the entire UNIVERSAL ECONOMIC RESOURCES on earth, space and below the earth. The earth is the Lord and everything in it. He created the mineral resources—oil, natural gas, gold, diamond, silver, precious stones and metals. God perfectly positioned them for humanity's consumption most importantly for His children redeemed by the blood of Jesus. God has the power to redirect and channel resources you needed at your door post.

*The first step towards building a sound and solid financial foundation is to believe and acknowledge God is the Source of your financial provisions beyond your job, organization, business or investment.* It is God who gives you the ability to acquire wealth. Had he not given you *"the ability"* you will not have those provisions.

ஐஐஐ

# "The first step towards building a sound and solid financial foundation is to believe and acknowledge God is the Source of your financial provisions beyond your job, organization, business or investment."

**Francis Herras**

ஐஐஐ

Listen closely to what God said in His Words.

> *"But <u>remember</u> the LORD your God, for it is he who gives you **THE ABILITY TO PRODUCE WEALTH**, and so confirms his covenant, which he swore to your ancestors, as it is today" (Deuteronomy 8:18 NIV, emphasis mine).*

> *"Remember the LORD your God. He is the one who gives you **POWER TO BE SUCCESSFULL**, in order to fulfill the covenant he confirmed to your ancestors with an oath." (Deuteronomy 8:18 NLT, emphasis mine).*

> *"But you shall remember the LORD your God, for it is <u>He who is giving</u> you **POWER TO MAKE WEALTH**, that He may confirm His covenant which He swore to your fathers, as it is this day" (Deuteronomy 8:18 NIV, emphasis mine).*

For those of you who are successful and have acquire so much wealth, remember it is God who gives you *"the ability to produce wealth."* The reason he entrusted you with success and wealth is so you can bless other people in need.

- ✓ Remember, God has given you "the power to *make* wealth."
- ✓ God has given you "the *power* to be successful."
- ✓ God has given you "the *ability* to produce wealth."

172

This is part of God's covenant with his people. God has gifted his children with an incredible *"power," "ability,"* to *"make"* wealth or become successful. *Success, prosperity and abundance are part of God's promised provisions for his children.*

❦❦❦

## "Success, prosperity and abundance are part of God's promised provisions for his children."

### Francis Herras

❦❦❦

*God is a wealthy God.* God is a rich God. God is a successful God. Remember, God owns the universe he has been running it since the beginning of time. He holds it in his hand. Everything in the universe is upon his disposal including you.

When trusting God and serving his purpose for his glory, he can channel the resources you needed and resources to carry out his designed purpose for your life.

In other words, when you acknowledge God as the Source of your financial provisions, you have the reason to succeed in life. Why? Because when you believe and acknowledge God as your Provider he empowers you with the *"ability"* to *"make"* and *"produce"* wealth. He unleashed upon your life an *"anointing"* to create wealth not just for self consumption but more for the advancement of His kingdom on earth.

Encapsulated in this *"ability"* is the ability to think creatively, to imagine, to plan and wisdom to make the plan happen. God has limitless ideas to create wealth for you. He is the Source of true wisdom and strategies for you rise above Status quo beyond normal to extraordinary successful person.

### ✓ Second Honor God with your Finances

God doesn't need your money he wants your heart's loyalty and total and unwavering faith and commitment to his promises. He is more

173

interested in the state of your heart than the state of your accounts. God wants to be *first* in your life which includes your finances. He wants supremacy in every areas of your life!

Jesus said "Love the Lord your God with all your *heart* and with all your *soul* and with all your *strength* and with all your *mind*; and, 'Love your neighbor as yourself" (Luke 10:27 NIV).

Your love to God must be superlative! Your devotion to God must be 100 percent. God must be at the core of your finances.

*"Bring the whole **TITHE** into the storehouse, that there may be food in my house. <u>Test me</u> in this," says the Lord Almighty, "and see if I will not throw <u>open the floodgates of heaven and pour out so much blessing</u> that there will not be room enough to store it" (Malachi 3:10 NIV, emphasis mine).*

The principle of *tithing* is part of God's economy. It's a proven principle that works for good to those who believe and practice it. As a matter-of-fact *tithing is the second step towards building a strong and solid financial foundation.*

*God's principles always work well.* God's intention behind the principle of tithing is to bring good to his children and to pour out his abundant provisions including finances. God design tithing to bring God's good to his children. It is not the money that God is after but the state of your heart. Tithing is a *test* of your loyalty, devotion and obedience to God in matters of provisions.

ℒℒℒ

# "Tithing is your upward momentum in building a strong financial foundation."

## Francis Herras

ℒℒℒ

*Tithing is your upward momentum in building a strong financial foundation.* When you build on God's ideas, principles and recommendations you are doing what is right and pleasing to God. You are honoring him. Giving generously unlocks the *"floodgates of heaven and pour so much blessings that there will not be room enough to store it."*

Tithing is God's promise to *"more than enough."*

Let me present to you two money problems first *"not enough money"* and second *"more than enough money."* Which problem do you prefer to have? Not enough money problems or more than enough money problem?

When you acknowledge God as the Source of your financial provisions and honor God with your finances by giving tithes (10 percent of your income) you are walking in obedience with God on your way to *"more than enough"* money problem. *You will always win when you work according to God's economic principle.* God's word, promises and principles laid in the Bible always works well for his children.

## I.   Redeeming the Time to Carry out your Purpose

Good works always reciprocate good feelings. Doing right makes you good. Utilizing your talents and gifts makes you a better person. Utilizing your time wisely to do your goals makes you more productive.

The challenge of maximizing time before and after work requires focus, discipline, daily planning and progress assessment each day. In my case before going to work at 9:00 I got up earlier at 5:00 in the morning for prayer, devotion and then either work on my dissertation edit my book for publishing. After work at 5:00 PM, do work out, jogging, planning and reading. These need focus to meet the outcomes that I foresee in advance - the picture I see for my life 5 to 15 years from now.

Redeeming the time is crucial for your personal growth, professional development and success. *It is what you put in your 24 hours time that makes the change not the time.* Time is neutral. Time doesn't change you. You cause the change. Time gives you a space and venue to make great things happen such as your goals. The question you and I must ask is what am I putting in my 24 hours time? You can be very busy but does not necessarily mean you are moving forward with momentum towards your defined outcomes with your purpose in life. This means you and I must evaluate and assess our daily activities at home and at work to sort out and rank only those things that move us towards our goals. Prioritizing is the name of the game in accomplishing your goals not elimination. You rank the most important things in your life! I call this my 5 Big Rock to give you an example.

❧❧❧

## "It is what you put in your 24 hours time that makes the change not the time. Time is neutral."

**Francis Herras**

❧❧❧

### J. My 5 Big Rock

### 1. God—relationship with God

- Prayer
- Study of God's Word
- Sunday Worship

### 2. Family life – relationship with my family

- Marriage
- Children
- Income
- Quality Vacation
- Annual review of earlier year goals to set up new goals
- Family devotion
- Regular family meeting updates and consultation of matters that are important to everyone
- Fun, healthy, productive activities
- Healthy and positive communication
- Positive affirmation
- Healthy food
- Increase savings, assets, investments and properties
- Zero debt

3. **Work—professional life**

- Build a positive relationship with other staff and managers
- Minister to residents, family and staff
- Inspire others engage in a positive conversation, inspirational email, music or training
- Journal and writing books

4. **Education—personal development**

- Publish my first book—Forward Momentum: The Art of Winning in Life
- Finish my doctoral dissertation
- Listen to educational audio for my personal growth and development
- Equip and prepare family members for success
- Connect with mentor
- Conduct a workshop, training and seminars around Canada and the world.

5. **Friends - social life**

- Fun activities
- Life Group

## UPWARD MOMENTION ACTION STEPS

*Write your answers on a clean sheet of paper.*

In your own words explain the distinction between responsibility and deserving. How are going to apply this in your own Christian life?

Do you deserve to exist and live a good life? Why?

Who is the key to your better future and why?

Where is the starting point of your success and why? Are you specific on your goals?

What is the first step towards building a sound financial foundation?

Do you believe and practice the principle of tithing?

What are your Big Rocks? Describe them?

# CHAPTER 4

# Humility Look Up to God-Given Future

### Success is something you Create, Develop and Make Happen

Have you ever wonder what makes one successful? What propels the 10% of the population to their success? Experts claim that the one percent (1%) is richer than the 99% of the world's population. According to Oxfam *the richest 1% now has more wealth than the rest of the world combined.*[59] Why is this? What makes the one percent richest people in the world unique that have become the talks, targets and envy of the majority? There has to be a reason for their humongous success.

What is it that puts them to where they are? Is it what they have become that put them to where they are now? We may not agree to what they've become and the handling they've taken through to become but they are where they want to be as a *result* of what they've become. The point I want to make in this case is that success is the result of what the one percent has become whether you agree or not to what they have become. What the one percent has become puts them to where they want to be. In other words, the more they become the more successful and wealthier they become. The 99 percent population may totally oppose their ways, values, philosophies, priorities, personality, attitudes, ways, greed and morality

---

[59] Oxfam. "An Economy for The 1%." January 18, 2016. https://www.oxfam.org/sites/www.oxfam.org/files/file_attachments/bp210-economy-one-percent-tax-havens-180116-en_0.pdf. January 8, 2018.

but the fact still remains the same—the one percent successful people of the world are products of what they have become. What they have become open up to various kinds of opportunities and great possibilities. What I am trying to show is one major contributing part that propels the richest and successful people in the world to where they are now. Their success did not just happen, it's neither a product of luck nor a product of chance but considerably a result of their hidden personal intent, motive or personality you might not agree. Please understand that I am not condoning evil ways neither corrupted belief nor evil philosophies. What I am trying to point out directly is that their success is a result of what they have become. They are successful and wealthy because of what they have become. They make success and wealth happens.

So what's the distinction between the one percent (1%) richest population and the ninety-nine percent (99%)? *I think the one percent makes wealth and success happens while the ninety-nine percent let things happen.*

Example, Bill Gates is successful because of what he has become as a person. Warren Buffett is successful because of what he has become. Donald Trump is successful because of what he has become. Here is the truth, you may not agree to what they have become and did but the fact still remains the same, in their case success has become a product of what they've become. Their success is a result of what they've become as a person. Their success is not a result of luck but a result of what they have become and the more they become the more successful they become.

Being a lawyer don't just happen by chance. It requires long years of studies of at least 8 years and then practice. A medicine doctor didn't just happen accidentally but a result of a choice of becoming a medical doctor. Then it opens up to opportunities to practice of serving people. The more the physician practice and serve the more they become. The more they specialized, become experts on a particular medical field they become wealthy and successful.

You see success is not something you pursue. Success is something you create, develop and make happen within you first. The more you develop yourself the more you become what you want to become then success follows you. Success is attracted to you because you have become what success has asked - becoming the person you want to be conducive to the principles of the Word of God.

The point is plain and simple. You've become an accountant first as a person and then you offer essential accounting service to people and corporations then they pay you according to your specialized service. The more you offer specialized service the more you are paid better. The better you are paid the more you got money and felt good of yourself, career, finances and business. In this case, success doesn't just happen. You make success happen of what you've become an accountant. The more you specialize the more you become the person you want to become the more opportunities and possibilities opens up for you. In this case, you've attracted wealth and success for yourself because you make yourself valuable in the society.

*Success is a result of what you've become.* Success is not something that you pursue. Success is something you create, develop and make happen in you. Success is the result of what you have become as a person. Success is something you've attracted of the person you've become. Meaning your being has attracted your doing. Your being has attracted the unlimited opportunities of doing service to the masses that leads to unprecedented wealth and success.

What I do now is a result of what I have become a clinical chaplain, a coach and a counselor. One thing for sure, I did not just end up as a chaplain or accidentally becomes a counselor. I am a product of my choice to become one. I have to go through a series of specialize studies at Foothills Hospital in Calgary (CPE) but before this was a degree in Theology, double master's degree in Pastoral Studies and Mission and now finishing up my doctoral study in clinical counseling. *In this case I keep pursuing to become the person God wants me to become.* The more I become the more opportunities open up for me to practice and offer service to the masses that leads me to unprecedented success on every side. My success in this case is a result of what I have become. I may not appreciate the degree of difficulties I've gone through but they have become ingredients of what I have become now healthcare chaplain, coach, business counselor and financial advisor.

## A. The Pull of the Future!

The art of winning is Jesus Christ at the core of your being no matter what! Jesus is your view from the top. You are made to win. You are design to win. Jesus is your invisible armor that shields you from the pangs of the enemies of your soul. You are born to spread your wings and soar like an eagle over the ferocious storms of life. *The view from the top is the realization that you are a winner in Christ Jesus.* The Christ in you and the Spirit in you overcomes evils, sickness, disease, trials, tribulations and temptations of life. But, this requires a complete and total trust and absolute surrender to Jesus Christ as your Lord, Savior and King! Jesus is your upward momentum in life.

You must *see* yourself a winner in Christ! You must see yourself victor in Christ! You must see yourself a blessing to others in Christ! You must see yourself the way God sees you — "more than a conqueror" overcoming the Goliath of your life.

*The upward momentum is Christ at the core of your being!* He is the foundation of everything in your life including your wealth and success. There is no real success outside of Christ. In Christ you are successful.

Aligning your *purpose* to God's purpose is your upward momentum in the field you are in at this moment. *Carrying out God's purpose in your life here on earth is success.* Upward momentum is moving forward to the future you've designed with a deep conviction that the vision in your spirit is what God wants you to do. Walking in God's call is not easy but knowing the pull of the future upon your life as an agent of change and blessings to others is a view from the top.

*Do you see and feel the pull of the future in your current condition?* You are designed to do better! Do you see you can become more to do more for God's glory? Do you have a true sense that you've become the person you wanted to be and have done the things you've desired to do in this life?

Certainly one must ask the right question to get the right answer. I think Christians are guilty of spiritualizing everything in life. Example quoting scripture *"And my God will meet all your needs according to the riches of his glory in Christ Jesus"* (Philippians 4:19 NIV). This verse is an absolute promise with conditions according to the context, pretext and post text of the passage when the apostle Paul said it to the believers in Philippians.

There is no doubt in my mind God always provides. Absolutely no doubt the infallibility of his Word and the reliability of everything He promised in the Bible.

*One must be walking in obedience to God's will to enjoy God's various provisions. God's blessings are conditional.*

৩৩৩

# "One must be walking in obedience to God's will to enjoy God's various provisions. God's blessings are conditional."

**Francis Herras**

৩৩৩

For the farmers, it's plowing their farm before planting seeds for a great harvest. Harvest doesn't just happen. Crop doesn't just by chance to grow. They grow because farmers invested great effort, time, energy, technology and money to make the harvest happen in the future. This is called the law of sowing and reaping. Whatever you sow you shall reap. *The idea is if you don't plant you don't reap.* If you did not plant, you should not expect to reap. You can't just tell the seed, seed grow! You must plant the seed in order for it to grow. Guess what, you always reap more than what you've planted. One apple seed bears more apple fruits. One corn seed bears more corn. You always reap more than what you sow the joy of sowing and reaping.

What if you did not sow or plant for your future? Will you harvest something in the future? What if you did not prepare and plan for your future? Will you arrive in the future you wanted to see? You can't just go in the bank and tell the teller, hey I need cash. The teller will ask your savings account if you say "No I don't." She'll tell you sorry I can't give you cash.

You see, you can't just go to the bank and ask for money if you did not save or put in money in a form of saving account. First you save to withdraw in the future in times of need. Whatever you save you can withdraw. It's your money. So if you did not save you don't expect to withdraw in the future and don't be surprised if you end up or arrived in the future you don't want to see.

## B. Anticipating your Future

> *"For I know the plans I have for you," declares the LORD, "plans*
> *to prosper you and not to harm you, plans to give you hope and*
> *a future. Then you will call on me and come and pray to me,*
> *and I will listen to you. You will seek me and find me when you*
> *seek me with all your heart" (Jeremiah 29:11-13 NIV).*

You must believe God has prepared a future for you but it doesn't mean passivity on your part. It means embracing the idea God has a plan to give you a good future. Your role is to discover your future today as you walk with God, listen and follow His guidance as you journey to the future He prepared for you. Intentional prayer, planning and goal setting are part of this journey as you press on towards your future. You must discipline yourself focus on your priorities and engage on healthy lifestyle to arrive to your desired future.

The truth is, everybody wants to know the future! Many efforts and methodologies have been done to know the future. The astrologers, the witches, the false prophets have tried to know and influence the future.

*Is it possible to understand and expect the future?* Is it even possible to influence or change the future—*your* future!

Yes, absolutely possible to change the future through the goals and actions we take in the present. Yes, definitely possible to influence our future by careful planning through a series of choices, decisions, actions we take and people we are associated with at present.

Our today will be the future. The now will be the tomorrow. If the now will be the future we must be sure "the now is a good one" because the now will influence our future outcomes. There are so many factors that might influence or change our future. For example – our health, choices, decisions, actions, habits, goals, visions and dreams to name a few.

♫♫♫

# "There are so many factors that might influence or change our future. For example – our health, choices, decisions, actions, habits, goals, visions and dreams to name a few."

**Francis Herras**

♫♫♫

## Marriage

Did your choice and decision to get married (5, 10, 15, 20 years) ago influence or change your future (today)? It did in so many ways would you agree? Did your spouse and children influence your future (today)?

## Career or Business

Did your decision to work or engage in business change your future (today)? Tremendously in so many ways! Your income impacts your lifestyle would you agree? What if you stop pursuing your dreams 10 or 15 years ago, would you be where you are at now?

## Migration

Did your choice and decision to migrate to Canada or USA influence or change your future (today)? 20 years ago you were still in the Philippines, India, Serbia, or Bangkok. Of course it does in so many ways right?

## Mortgage

Did your decision to buy a house in Calgary affected, influence or change your future (today)? How is your lifestyle now comparing to your lifestyle back in your country of origin?

*The bottom line is your choices, decisions, actions and habits today will influence and change the landscape of your future!*

Here is a fact: 20 years ago was your 'present', that 'present' became your past, and your 'now' (10 years) will be your future. This implies that you and I must pay attention to the choices, decisions, actions and habits that we make in the present to have a good or better future.

## C. Where are you now?

The first step in learning your *future* is to look at your *past* and your *present* because they are bases from which you will catapult yourself into the future you want.

PAST – PRESENT FUTURE

Your *knowledge* of your own life will prepare you for exploring your *plausible* future. Here are areas you need to know about yourself.

- Your origin
- Your dreams
- Your Vision
- Your Purpose
- Your decision making process
- Your mindset
- Your choices
- Your habits
- Your practice
- Your career
- Your leadership
- Your attitude
- Your priorities

All the above will influence and play a major role in shaping your future!

# DECISIONS, CHOICES, ACTIONS

- **Marriage**
- **Career or Business**
- **Migration to Canada**
- **Your first House**

> The bottom line is your choices, decisions,
> actions and habits will influence and change
> your future!

Please remember this …

- When you have a *vision*, a *picture* in your mind of the future you wish to be ten years from now, you have created a *long-term view* of your life.
- You may not be able to follow a straight line or smooth sailing journey from present to your future, but when you have a *vision* of what you want in life, that vision will give you a target *destination* so you constantly moving forward. This is your forward momentum.

*Remember, your vision will be your destination!*

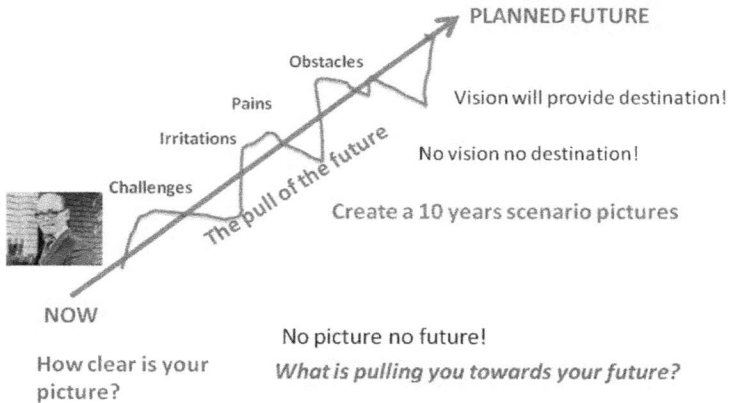

## D. Your Vision is your Destination

The route to the future definitely will not be straight line as described in the picture. Life's journey has never been and will never be a straight line.

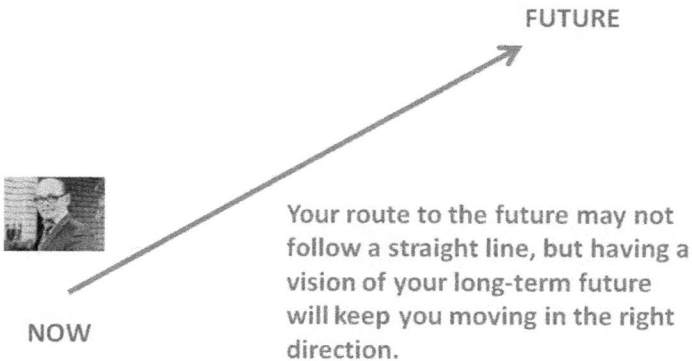

A perfect illustration is a stochastic line consists of lower lows and higher highs. Your journey to the future will not be smooth sailing it's going to be like a stocks market indicator lines that you must navigate and take control if you want to arrive in your desired future but having a vision of your long-term future will keep you moving forward in the right direction.

There are things you must do to design your future.

- ✓ DREAM your future. You are made to think and imagine your future.
- ✓ DECIDE what you want for your future.
- ✓ DRAW the picture of your future in mind and paper. Remember, no picture no future.
- ✓ DETERMINE what you have to do to get there. Be sharp on your S.M.A.R.T Goals.
- ✓ DO it cautiously and courageously.
- ✓ DECIPLINE yourself to make it happen.
- ✓ DEVELOP yourself consistently.

*You must create your future by designing your future today.* The way to do it is spend plenty of time in payer with God who has prepared a future for you. You must spend quality time thinking, planning and prioritizing to make your future a good one!

≈≈≈

## "You must create your future by designing your future today."

### Francis Herras

≈≈≈

The slide will show you how you can plan and think of your future for example in terms of saving money but the idea is applicable in any goals.

Probability: The likelihood of something happening, likely to occur

Possibility: A thing that may happen, or be the case

Plausibility: Credible, believable, worthy of approval, appearance of truth
And reason

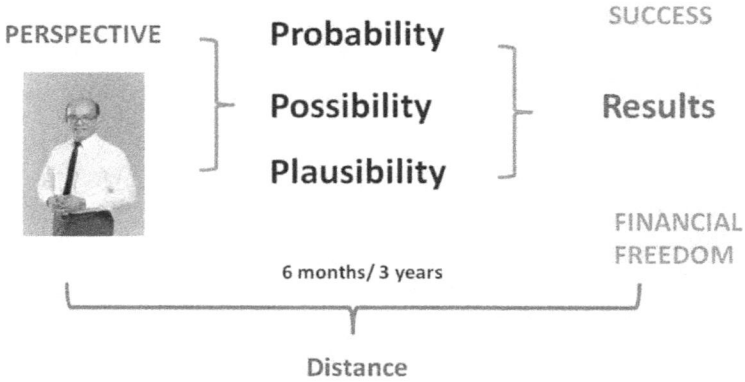

I wonder if this idea can be applied in lifestyle, career, business or family.

*Is it possible to transition from your present view to the view from the top?* Can you embrace the view from the top? I discover *perspective* will change you from the inside first. Remember my story a 5 minutes drive change of location and elevation creates a life changing experience, a view from the top experience!

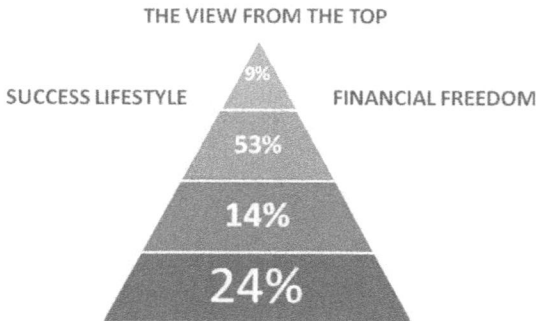

THE VIEW FROM THE TOP

SUCCESS LIFESTYLE    FINANCIAL FREEDOM

9%

53%

14%

24%

**UPWARD MOMENTION ACTION STEPS**

*Write your answers on a clean sheet of paper.*

What makes the one percent (1%) richest people
in the world uniquely successful? There must be a
reason. Can you expound and give examples?

What is your view of success? Do you consider yourself successful?
Please elaborate your answer how you can apply them in your life.

How do you see yourself? Describe your perspective of yourself
and how your perspective is influencing your success.

Do you believe God has prepared a better for you? Why?

Can you virtually describe the future you wish to
arrive and see five or ten years from now?

What is the first step in learning and planning your future?

How do you understand "no picture no future" and
"no vision no destination?" Please explain your answer
in connection with your own context in life.

# CHAPTER 5

# Humility Cures Pride and Attracts Success

*"Blessed is the man who walks not in the counsel of the wicked, nor stands in the way of sinners, nor sits in the seat of scoffers; but his delight is in the law of the LORD, and on his law he meditates day and night. He is like a tree planted by streams of water that yields its fruit in its season, and its leaf does not wither. In all that he does, he prospers."* (Psalm 1:1-3 ESV)

Every thought, imaginations, feelings, desires, dreams, visions, goals, words, plans that exalt itself up against the knowledge of God must be subdued. *Inner strongholds* must be dismantled including limiting beliefs that doesn't help you become successful in every areas of life.

Every stronghold in your *mind and sub-conscious mind* that hinders your spiritual growth, prosperity, destiny and carrying out purpose must come be subjected to the Lordship of Christ. Every motive, desires and inclination of rebellion against God's holiness and personality must be subdued.

Every knee, every tongue must confess that Jesus is Lord to the glory of the Father. *"That at the name of Jesus every knee should bow, in heaven and on earth and under the earth, and every tongue acknowledge that Jesus Christ is Lord, to the glory of God the Father" Philippians 2:10-11 NIV).* This includes fallen angels, demons, and evil spirits that entice God's people to sin to separate them from God. Every form of aggression, violence, rebellion, disharmony, depression, fear, a worry, a feeling of uncertainty, and a feeling of insecurity or inferiority must come down, subdued and kneel before Jesus who is the only Ultimate Power that can destroy them to set his people free from those strongholds.

Every form of evil, a wicked and lustful imagination is a stronghold that must surrender to the authority of Jesus. *Your mind is meticulously designed to imagine good and godly things, things to bring you closer to God and to unleash your highest kingdom potentials in providing service to humanity.*

The mind must be *transformed and renewed* by reading, studying and meditating on God's Word that has the power to cleanse, purify and sanctify the mind. *The mind must be renewed and nourished by the Word of God led by the regenerated human spirit.* Your spirit can be saved and regenerated but if your mind is not fed, nourished and renewed by God's Word it creates *internal conflict* or disunity within yourself. Your mind must be subdued saturated by God's Word for *your spirit* to channel ideas, thoughts, visions, dreams, goals and plans your spirit received from the Holy Spirit that dwells in you. Your *mind and your spirit* must be in harmony in order for you to grow and move forward to life. The source of nutrition of your mind and spirit is the Word of God. The Word of God is the menu and the dessert of your mind and spirit which will influence your behavior, priorities and lifestyle.

⚘⚘⚘

## "Renewing your mind means renewing your life and behavior."

**Francis Herras**

⚘⚘⚘

*Renewing your mind means renewing your life and behavior.* Transforming your mind with God's Word means transforming your life, behavior and priorities. You change your mind; you change your life. You change your mind; you change your behavior. You change your mind; you change your future and destiny. The issue is not just to change your mind but renewing and transforming your mind with God's Word so you become the product change - transformed by the incorruptible seed of the Word of God. *Being change by God Himself is your upward momentum that builds your forward momentum to win in life!*

To change your behavioral outcomes, you must change the way you think; you must think well; you must reason well; ponder and show well in every aspects of your being. Behavioral outcomes are the product of an *inner change in the spirit and soul* (mind). Inner change reflects outer change. For positive growth to continue, negativity must be eradicated; negative ideas must be subdued; negative thoughts must be eliminated; negative desires words must stop; negative pictures in mind must be changed into a positive; negative feelings must renounce; negative perception and projection of yourself must replaced with positive ones; *everything that limits you and pull away from your highest potentials and walk with God must be demolished.*

♥♥♥

## "Everything that limits you and pull away from your highest potentials and walk with God must be demolished."

**Francis Herras**

♥♥♥

Every good things, positive things, ideas, plans, visions and dreams that you think God placed in your spirit and mind must rise above your weaknesses and limitations. Everything that comes from God, kingdom agendas, and God glorifying plans must arise. Everything that comes from the Kingdom of God must shine and everything that comes from the darkness must be disperse and destroyed. Let God arise and let his enemies be scattered in every areas dimension of your my being — spiritually, emotionally, mentally and physically!

Let God arise in your ***spirit*** born of the incorruptible seed of God! Let God arise in your ***inner sanctum*** created in God's image and likeness! Let God saturate your ***conscience*** with the Spirit of Truth, Advocate and

Comforter! Let God shine in and through your will so you can do His will in your life, marriage, family, ministry and business.

Let God saturate your **body** and five senses — seeing, hearing, touching, smelling, and tasting! Let God senses be your senses. Let every form of negativity and evil tendencies be demolished in your five senses because you are a living sacrifice to God to carry out his original intent for my life.

Let God saturate your **soul**! Let every choice, reason, wish, feelings, emotions, ideas of life and future align with His. Let God arise in your whole being and his enemies be scattered while you journey in this fallen world guided by His Word and His Holy Spirit!

Remember …

- Humility Attracts Productivity
- Humility Guarantees Promotion
- Humility Leads to Prosperity
- Humility Attracts Success

## A. A journey to experience God Requires Humility

*Christian life is a journey with God.* It is a journey to *experience* the Person of God in the spirit of humility till we reach our final destiny in eternity. Experiencing the presence of God is one great challenge among believers. Why is this? Our hearts and minds are occupied with so many good things - life, self, family, business, plans and future.

Our minds are constantly bombarded with ideas both good and wrong. Our hearts and spirit is choked and suffocated with things and information that takes our time to seek God and move us away from accomplishing his purpose for our lives. Our minds are overflowing with lots of "stuff" that it lives no room for God.

People are overwhelmed, overworked, over the limits. As a result, everything they do had no impact and no meaning. They're just doing things. They're just doing the "stuff." They just exist aimlessly. This leads to discouragement, disappointments, frustration, anger and depression. As a result, they suffer lots of unnecessary things in life because they've detached themselves from God in the journey. They've declared independence by embracing the "things" and "stuff" of life.

It's either were so ahead of God or way behind God. In other words, we're not walking with God in the journey of life. We're walking with ourselves. Yes, God is still there. His promise was He will never leave us nor forsake us. *"Be strong and courageous. Do not be afraid or terrified because of them, for the LORD your God goes with you; he will never leave you nor forsake you" (Deuteronomy 31:6 NIV)*. But if we chose to leave him or chose to journey without him, his presence is still available for us. The right thing to do is look behind or look ahead and ask God's forgiveness for doing it ourselves (pride) and then humbly continue walking with God in the journey of life as you carry out your purpose.

## B. The Heart's Cry of a Warrior - the Apple of God's Eye

*"I am weary with my moaning; every night I flood my bed tears; I drench my couch with my weeping. My eye wastes away because of all my foes." (Psalm 6:6 ESV)*.

King David, God's chosen to reign, the apple of God's eye was in great pain pleading for God's grace *"for I am languishing" (Psalm 6:2 ESV)*. David was seeking God's healing, *"for my bones are troubled" (Psalm 6:2 ESV)*; *"my soul is greatly troubled" (Psalm 6:3 ESV)*. In verse four David prays for deliverance from his enemies, *"deliver my life; save me for the sake of your steadfast love" (Psalm 6:4 ESV)*. Only a humble political figure can do this before God opposite to the 21st century humanist political mindset.

King David was greatly troubled deep in his soul. He fears his life. He felt the piercing opposition of his ungodly political enemies. He sees his limitations as a human being. He cries and pours out his heart and mind out to God who called him to be King of Israel. I wonder how many politicians in key government position both in North America, USA and around the world are doing what David did – calling upon God for His Divine intervention. If you are a politician learn from David. Listen to his heart and see if you can identify with him.

King David calls upon God in trouble. Calling upon God is the right thing for a politician to do especially when in trouble.

The good thing with David was he did not sugar quote what he feels about himself and his plight he sees it as opportunity call upon God. He pours out what he feels. He was honest in what he feels about himself and his condition he was facing. He recognizes his *emotional state* — *"languishing," "my bones are troubled," "my soul is greatly troubled," "I am weary with my moaning; every night I flood my bed tears; I drench my couch with my weeping."*

David was honest to acknowledge his *enemies impact* on his life *"of all my foes."* David was feeling the piercing of darkness in his soul and bones! David's foe has a tremendous *psychological* impact on him. David was overwhelmed with what he hears, witness and experience as a leader. David sees the reality of evil working through people who are against him and against God's plan in his leadership domain.

David's call to God was not an indicator of weakness but a prayer of a political warrior. David was God's political warrior! His prayer was a recognition of his need of God's help to face his opponents. Listen to his cry, *"O Lord, rebuke me not in your anger"* (Psalm 6:1 ESV), *"deliver my life,"* Psalm 6:2a, *"save me v.2b" "for the Lord has heard the sound of my weeping v. 8," "the Lord has heard my plea; the Lord accepts my prayer v.9."* Here, David has the assurance that God has heard his plea and prayer for deliverance because he put his heart out to God in total dependence with *what God can do to him and his enemies.* Here, *David finds his encouragement in God alone.* David was assured and gain strength from God after pouring his heart out in prayer with honesty and sincerity. This was David upward momentum!

I think David has showed us that it's okay to cry and pour out our heart to God when in deep trouble as a political leader. I've learned that it's totally okay to cry as a child of God when you are feeling the piercing of the darkness in your soul and the piercing of the people who oppose God's plan and purpose. *It is totally okay to recognize the psychological, mental, emotional, physiological impact caused by God's enemies to seek God's help. It is absolutely okay to be you in God's presence.* This is your upward momentum. It's totally okay to be vulnerable and transparent in the presence of God while you are going through difficult times; it's okay to encourage yourself with who God is and what he can do to you, and your enemies.

❧❧❧

# "It is totally okay to recognize the psychological, mental, emotional, physiological impact caused by God's enemies to seek God's help. It is absolutely okay to be you in God's presence."

**Francis Herras**

❧❧❧

## C. How God See His Children in Christ

How God sees me is my identity. *My true identity and meaning is defined by God my Creator.* My real identity is described in the Bible the infallible Word of God. I am what God says I am. *I am not what people say I am.* My true identity originated from God when he "fearfully and wonderfully" made me in my mother's womb and breath upon me the breath of life. God's breath of Life made me a living soul. His life gives me life through the agency of my parents. *His life defines me* when God breathe the breath of life in me, his unconditional love, goodness, peace, joy, righteousness, personality, and intelligence flows through Him on me while I am still in my mother's womb. *He breathes me His life. Life to life!*

I am alive in my mother's womb with God-given life, His life my life in my fetus state. *My origin is God Himself. My true meaning is the meaning He placed upon me when He created me.* I belong to God and He belongs to me. Although both my parents are long gone, I am not alone because I still have my real heavenly Father who formed me in my mother's womb and who allow me to exist and live on earth he created. I trust in God's plan and purpose for my life as well as for my household. *I understand God believes in me more than I believe in myself.* His plan and purpose is bigger than what I dreamed or imagine. *Real life begins in eternity with God.* This is "life above the sun" which Solomon struggles to understand his "life under the sun."

God's life goes out to Adam when he created him - the *"image and likeness"* of God imparted to Adam. It was God's life that makes Adam unique, magnificent creature. It was the life of God that makes Adam humanly perfect, intelligent, rational moral being.

The first thing that Adam saw and experienced in the Garden of Eden was God the Father Himself. In the same manner, the first thing a newly born baby feels, hear is his/her parents. God brought life on earth His creation but more so He brought human life through Adam the first human being on earth.

*Man is eternal being made by God.* Man will continue to live in eternity at the culmination of his earthly life. Those who accept and embrace Christ redemptive work on Calvary will be with Jesus in heaven to enjoy eternal fellowship with the Triune God. Those that reject Jesus and his redemptive works and his Gospel will spend Christless eternity; forever separated from the presence of the Triune God into eternal damnation in hell a place that God prepares for Satan, demons and false prophets.

So, extremely essential to examine what the Word of God says to gain a solid perspective on how I look myself and how God sees me or think of me. This examination will create an alignment of my perspective to God's view of me. *To see myself the way God sees me will bring me into a deeper walk with God. To understand the way God think of me will dramatically alter any false belief or notion that have been channeled to me of my earlier generations.*

☙☙☙

## "To understand the way God think of me will dramatically alter any false belief or notion that have been channeled to me of my earlier generations."

### Francis Herras

☙☙☙

*I must see the way God sees me.* I must think the way God thinks of me. I must see life the way God sees it. I must see the world the way God view it. I must see relationship the way God sees it. I must see marriage and family the way God sees it. I must see riches, wealth, money, success and accomplishments the way God sees it. Why you asked? The answer is plain and simple. Life was His idea. Marriage and relationships was His idea. Riches, wealth, money, success and accomplishments were His idea. So, important I see the real reason and purpose behind those things. I must see them the way God sees them. This is a true perspective and the highest form of worldview in reference to God. *It is a belief that sees God at the core of life,* relationship, marriage, riches, wealth, success and accomplishments. *A belief or worldview deeply founded on God Himself.*

Since God is the author of everything that exists in the universe including human beings he must have a good reason for creating them. My highest goal then is to align my reasoning, spirit, soul and body to that perspective so that I may live a life according to his design.

My true identity is found in Christ a reminder of who I am. Listen to what the Word of God says who you are.

## I am faithful

"Paul, an apostle of Christ Jesus by the will of God, To *God's holy people* in Ephesus, **the faithful** in *Christ Jesus*" (Ephesians 1:1 NIV, emphasis mine)

The apostle Paul sees Christ follower in Ephesians as *"God's holy people"* and *"the faithful in Christ Jesus."* This is an affirmation of who you are in Christ. In Christ you are made holy. His holiness becomes your holiness by virtue of your belief in him. Christ's holiness was imparted on you the day you accepted Jesus as your Lord and Savior your life. In Christ you are holy, purified, sanctified, forgiven and washed by his blood. In Christ you become the righteousness of God. This is how the Scripture says who you are. This is how God says to you and me.

## I am God's child

*"Yet to all who did receive him, to those who believed in his name, he gave the right to become children of God"* (John 1:12 NIV)

## I am Christ's friend

> *"I no longer call you servants, because a servant does not know his master's business. Instead, I have called you friends, for everything that I learned from my Father I have made known to you." (John 15:15 NIV)*

## I am a member of Christ's Body

> *"Now you are the body of Christ, and each one of you is a part of it." (1 Corinthians 12:27 NIV)*

## I am assured all things work together for good

> *"And we know that in all things God works for the good of those who love him, who have been called according to his purpose." (Romans 8:28 NIV)*

## I am confident that God will perfect the work He has begun in me

> *"Being confident of this, that he who began a good work in you will carry it on to completion until the day of Christ Jesus" (Philippians 1:6 NIV).*

## I am a citizen of heaven

> *"But our citizenship is in heaven. And we eagerly await a Savior from there, the Lord Jesus Christ" (Philippians 3:20 NIV).*

**I am born of God and the evil one cannot touch me**

> *"We know that anyone born of God does not continue to sin; the One who was born of God keeps them safe, and the evil one cannot harm them" (1 John 5:18 NIV).*

**I am blessed in the heavenly realms with every spiritual blessing**

> *"Praise be to the God and Father of our Lord Jesus Christ, who has blessed us in the heavenly realms with every spiritual blessing in Christ" (Ephesians 1:3 NIV).*

---

### UPWARD MOMENTION ACTION STEPS

*Write your answers on a clean sheet of paper.*

What strongholds in your mind hinder you to prosper, grow spiritually and carry out your purpose in life? Name them and renounce them in Jesus Name. (Example: pride)

What is the most effective way of renewing your mind to transform your life? Please explain.

Explain "How God sees me is my identity" and how this perspective will change and attract success in your life.

Do you believe man is an eternal being made by God and will continue to live in eternity at the culmination of his earthly life? How is this going to influence your lifestyle today?

---

# CONCLUSION

### Fight to Win the Good Fight of Faith!

*"This charge I commit to you, son Timothy, according to the prophecies previously made concerning you, that by them you may wage the good warfare, having faith and a good conscience, which some having rejected, concerning the faith have suffered shipwreck, of whom are Hymenaeus and Alexander, whom I delivered to Satan that they may learn not to blaspheme." (1 Timothy 1:18 NKJV)*

*As Christ's follower we are in a battle every single day.* One form of this battle is an *internal battle.* We fight to win not to lose even if it cost our lives. We fight for our faith courageously. We fight for our God-given purpose relentlessly. We fight for the accomplishment of our dreams, preservation of our marriage, family, and everything that God has provided for us. We fight for the truth against lies of the enemy of our soul. *We fight for what is morally correct against what is politically right.* We fight for greatness against the mediocrity. We fight for love against selfishness; hope against despair; prosperity against poverty; unity against disunity; healthy communication against abusive communication; productivity against passivity; generosity against hoarding; hospitality against stinginess; prayer against prayerlessness; devotion and meditation against neglect of God's Word. If we don't fight, we will end up push back and ultimately crushed and defeated. This is not God's plan for his children. You have everything to win in life's battle. You have total access to God's unlimited arsenal at your disposal to win your battle. But you must fight a good fight of faith in partnership with God to win your battle in life at this very moment.

*The battle within us is the most fatal battle that Christian will ever*

203

*face.* This battle is worse than Nepal earthquake, Dessert Storm War, Tsunami or any natural catastrophe that is happening around the globe. This internal battle had put millions of lives in the mental institutions, produce drug addicts, dysfunctional families, suicides, codependency, broken families and marriages, wreck business, wreck organizations and churches.

What are you fighting for these days? What are you fighting for that is holding you back to move forward and grow spiritually? What are you fighting for that is keeping you unproductive? What are you fighting for that is controlling your life or keeping you in bondage doing the things that breaks the heart of God? Are you fighting with God the right battle for yourself?

So what are you fighting? Is your faith worth fighting? Is the sanctity of your marriage worth fighting? Is your family worth fighting? Is the church of Christ worth fighting? Are moral values and philosophies grounded in God's Word worth fighting? Is your health worth fighting? Is your garden worth fighting for against weeds, bugs and insects? Of course! That is why you spray the grass, plants and flowers with weeds control. You want everything that kills and destroy life or in this case your garden away! If you don't protect your garden and fight against insect, they'll invade and take over your garden. So you must defend your garden; you must defend your crop; defend your health from unhealthy food and activities; defend your mind from thoughts that corrupts your life; defend your property and belongings from a thief and intruders. If you don't they'll come and take away everything you've got and destroy your life. You must defend yourself from impulsive behaviors and responses such as overspending your hard earned money on something you don't need. You must protect yourself against poverty now to have a better future when you retire by frugally saving for your future income retirement. You must save now to enjoy later. Or enjoy now suffer later. The choice is yours.

You must protect your finances and investments wisely. If you don't you will end up having nothing or bankrupt. Be a frugal steward of God's blessings so one day you will be in a position to bless others.

*Fight for your God-given purpose!* Fight for your dreams! Fight for your values! Fight for your future! Fight for your marriage and family. Fight for everything that destroys life. Most importantly fight for your faith and what you believe God and His Word the Bible!

**This I Believe! (Hebrews 11:1)**

Let me share with you what I personally believe for the coming years and beyond: ***All for the glory of God!*** All for King Jesus and advancement of His Kingdom in the hearts of men, women and children! A year without limits in doing ministry! A year for greater things; greater love, peace and joy; greater heights of kingdom opportunities to climb; limitless meaningful ministry open doors that will make a positive influence among young lives; fearless and courageous year; a forward momentum year; a year where dreams come true; a year of unprecedented miracles in my finances, possessions and properties. A year of the Lord's favor from financial institutions and professional organization I am connected with personally and professionally.

I believe my family is abundantly provided by the economy of God's kingdom where no economic recession. God's prosperity continuously overflows without ending in my life as well as family and the generation to come!

I believe the trajectory of my life is poised to complete my purpose, effort, energy, action, activities; decisions are girded towards the realization of my ultimate design in life including my four children as well.

*I exist for the glory of God alone!* I exist for Jesus! I exist for the advancement of His Kingdom through the proclamation of the Gospel! I exist to carry out God's purpose for my life. I belong to God and He belongs to me in Christ Jesus my Savior, Healer, Sanctifier and coming King!

**Life Creates You**

Life in itself is perfect. Life is alive. Life develops and multiplies. You do not create life, life creates you. You are subjected to life. Life is a precious gift from God when He breathes upon you the breath of life while you are in your mother's womb. The sperm became a living soul. The union of the liquid substance (sperm) and the human spirit design by God transformed to an embryo, becomes a baby, then born. You are a product of a life that God has embedded in the human DNA. You are a fruit of human "seed" that became a living soul because of God's breath of life.

The "human seed" has been designed of God to pro-create to raise a godly family, a "godly seed" or "a godly offspring" that honor the Author and the Giver of life.

At the core of an apple are hidden seeds but when planted can potentially transform into a fruit bearing apple tree producing more fruits; in the same manner, at the very core of your being embedded "the human seed" to pro-create and multiply godly offspring on earth.

You are given a "gift of life" in you to produce and multiply with God's blessings way back in the Garden of Eden. God's life is planted in you. It is totally up to you how you will exercise your free will to raise an offspring you wanted to produce—godly offspring or ungodly offspring. The gift of life is within your discretion to use it for your good and God's glory.

God is the Source of human life. Life did not cause life *God caused life* (mankind and universe). Human race is the result of life God has caused. Human beings reproduce and multiply as a result of God's design. God has blessed the human race with the life to live; but, the choice to live the lifestyle is totally according to man's free will or freedom to choose or preference. Within man is life given by God yet live out according to man's judgment and choice.

As free will individual you have a choice to live life for your good, the good of humanity, carry out your purpose for God's glory. Furthermore, as a rational being you have a choice to live life for yourself apart from God. The choice is yours. Bear in mind both life and free will are gifts from God. God has given you freedom to exercise choice and lifestyle to choose whom you will serve. The question now is, will you live your life for God and exercise your freedom of choice for Jesus?

Your life's development, growth and progress are influenced by the choices you made. Your life now is a direct result of your choices years ago. Your work, your house, your cars, and your clothes are the results of exercising your choices. The image that you project; the personality you display are results of your personal choices. Things in your life did not just happen. They happen because you make them happen. Your choices made them happen.

*Life and choice goes hand in hand.* Your life grows and will continue according to the choices you made.

Life will impact your choices. But, life creates you as you make choices. As you continue to make choices life flourished. Life is affected and driven by your choices. Life is neutral, a gift from God but dependent on your choices for godly outcomes. Daily decision has to be made for your life to progress and move forward. *Life can either draw the best out of you or draw the beast out you; both effects are caused by your choices regardless of your reality.* Life follows choices and choices are made by you.

❧❧❧

## "Life can either draw the *best* out of you or draw the *beast* out you; both effects are caused by your choices regardless of your reality."

### Francis Herras

❧❧❧

### Fork Roads of Life

What do you do when you are faced with great opportunities that entail relocation, lots of traveling, and higher expenses, away from your family but better salary?

*Life brings us plenty of fork roads.* Those fork roads need thoughtful and prayerful decisions and smart planning. Others, requires simple and practical wisdom.

I think one major challenge people face in pursuit of their ultimate purpose in life is moving forward to the future God has prepared for them. Discerning God's good, pleasing and perfect is easier said than done.

In my case, one of my major fork roads was a choice between working in Lethbridge (two-in-a-half hours to drive from home) or Edmonton (three hours drive from home) when I was offered a good paying position by my director.

I just move in to my new rental house in Lethbridge and sign for a one year lease contract. Things are looking good at work. I have a nice office on both facilities that I work with as a chaplain. Everything is within 15 minutes driving range. Life is simpler and slower in Lethbridge comparing to Calgary.

My major struggle was being away five days a week from my family and the five hours drive. So I decided to stay in Lethbridge to make things simple plus it's closer to home than Edmonton but still need sacrifices on my part.

*Life is precious. It is a gift to cherish. It is a precious gift to flourish.* You are responsible for your life. God has given you everything to make your life meaningful and significant on this planet. You are given everything you need to succeed in spite of the fork roads life will bring.

❧❧❧

## "Life is precious. It is a gift to cherish. It is a precious gift to flourish."

### Francis Herras

❧❧❧

In Christ you are made complete. He paid the great price on the cross for your redemption, deliverance and salvation. In Christ you are free from guilt and condemnation. In Christ you are justified and sanctified by His Spirit that dwells in you now. In Christ you are made valuable so you can value and appreciate your life and value other people's life.

*In Christ you are not alone facing your major fork roads.* You are always surrounded with God's presence. God did not design you to be alone in times of difficulties. He is with you always to give you wisdom to choose what is good and pleasing as you are confronted with major fork roads of life.

In this life you were never alone. From the day you were conceived you were never alone. God's eye was upon you when you were conceived. He did not take off his eyes upon you. He is watching you always *"I will never leave you nor forsake you."*

You were surrounded with people who love you such as your parents and love ones. God did not forsake you but you did many times. He protected and preserved you in times of your deepest needs and hurts. God is always there for you. But you must hear his voice to make the right decision especially when facing challenging fork roads. *Hearing God's voice is the key to moving forward and success in life.*

.๑.๑.๑

## "Hearing God's voice is the key to moving forward and success in life."

### Francis Herras

.๑.๑.๑

Pause and pray this prayer.

> "Oh, Lord Jesus, help me to see things the way you see it and help me to make decisions the way you make decisions in my current circumstance. Let your peace beams upon me and let your joy bubble up in me. Let your mind be my mind and let your passion be my passion. Let your prayers be my prayers and your steps be my steps! Come, Lord Jesus fill my life with the freshness of your life that my life flourish. Let your life shines through me. Let your presence and power so visible in my life and everything I do so I can become a good influence among many. Lord Jesus be at the core of my being, family and everything I do; use me to stir up the spirit of the nations to awaken their passion, dreams, purpose and meaning. Empower me with your Spirit to create a tidal wave of godly passion across the globe; empower me to awaken the nations soul and points them to you; empower me to speak to proclaim with clarity, boldness, wisdom, and humility a message that will alter belief that pulls people away from you; anoint me to live a holy life to travel around the world to proclaim your gospel, prosperity and abundance.

Lord Jesus, please lead me to the next level of ministry; take me to the next page of my life according to your original intent when you made me in my mother's womb. Remove every covering that blinds me so I can see clearly your direction. Lead me to the right decision to make. Help me to do it with peace and confidence in you. Give me an undivided heart and sharpen my spiritual discernment so that I may only choose your leading and prompting, I ask this in the precious name of Jesus my Lord and Savior. Amen!

## CONCLUSION

**In conclusion**, the upward momentum is consciously living life in the *presence* of God. Intentionally developing a lifestyle that recognizes God's presence will radically change you inwardly, sharpen your eternal perspective. In the presence of God things becomes clearer—your purpose, meaning, happiness and priorities in life.

The idea of willfully living a humble life is to be in *partnership* with God in the journey of life here on earth. Partnership with God is your assurance, security and safety as you forge into the complex jungle of life carrying out God-given purpose until your last breath. With God you can do great things to influence millions of people for Jesus. When you allow God's presence to work in your life, you become an agent of transformation for God's kingdom upon the lives of many.

.•.•.•.

# "The Person of God is my personal and ministry trade mark."

### Francis Herras

.•.•.•.

*The Person of God is my personal and ministry trade mark.* His presence at work in my life identifies who I am and what I do. God's call or partnership with me is what I do—advancing His kingdom into the hearts of people. Jesus Christ the King defines my personal and ministry identity. His manifest presence at work is my ministry logo. In other words, people witness and experience Jesus in what I do. Meaning God is known, seen, experienced by people in my ministry.

*God's presence is my inward and forward momentum in life.* So if you want to build or create momentum to carry out your purpose, you must begin to humble yourself in His presence with a repentant heart. You begin every moment of your life in God's presence. Your moment with God is your momentum in marriage, family, work and ministry or whatever you advance in His kingdom. If you've lost your momentum but want to regain it back, you must become a person of God's presence! You must become a dweller in God's presence until your life is consumed with His holiness, purity, love, authority and power, until you become what God wants you to be.

There is only one way to regain lost spiritual momentum—in the presence of Jesus in the spirit of repentance embracing His plan for your life. To build or rebuild spiritual, psychological and physiological momentum is to soak yourself in the presence of God, being still to Him intimately, to be inwardly transformed and filled by His Spirit. In the presence of Jesus until nothing else truly matter but Him alone this idea is your supernatural momentum that will shake the world for Jesus!

The Bible in Exodus 33 shows the sin of the Hebrew people has committed against God the sin of idolatry which God hates. This happens right after God delivers them from slavery in Egypt for more than 400 years through Moses' leadership back up with God's power. Instead of worshipping God who loved, cared and rescued them from bondage of slavery and abuses, they decided to make their own god out of gold. God was not pleased with what they did as a result God was angry because of their hard heart and spiritual blindness.

In Exodus we see Moses before God confessed the sin of his people. He was interceding on behalf of his people. Listen closely. *"Oh, these people have committed a **great sin**, and **made** themselves a **god of gold**!" (Exodus 32:31 NKJV, emphasis mine).* Here we see Moses not only acknowledge the sin of the people he was leading but show and stand in the gap for God's forgiveness. *"Yet now, if you will forgive their sin—but if not, I pray, **blot*** *me out of your book which you have written."* (Exodus 32:32 NKJV, *emphasis mine).* What a prayer! Moses was willing to trade-in his eternal destiny for the sake of his own people. He was willing his name be blotted out from the book of life for the forgiveness of his people. But God did not agree with what Moses asked because he was innocent. God's response to his prayer was, *"Whoever has sinned against me, I will blot him out of my book"* (Exodus 32:32 NKJV). In other words, God was after the people who committed the sin. Because of the sin of idolatry the people committed there was a change in God's plan. In Exodus 32:34, God changed his plan. Instead of going with people, he sends His angel as a proxy to go with them in their journey to the Promised Land. God's presence at that particular setting was not favorable for the people because of the great sin they've committed. God's presence might consume them to their destruction, so He sends a proxy to go with them in their journey to the Promised Land. *"My angel shall go before you"* (Exodus 32:34 NKJV). In other words, I will not be with you but my eyes are on you. As a matter of fact the Lord plagued them. *"So the Lord **plagued** the people because of what they did with calf which Aaron made"* (Exodus 32:35 NKJV, *emphasis mine). We see clearly God withdraw His presence from His people because of their sins. The sin of idolatry created the gap.*

God hates idolatry because it replaces and reduces Him into a manmade statue that can't move, talk, understand, see or hear. God hates sins, but the Israelites had committed a grievous sin that violates the first commandment.

> ² *"**I am the Lord your God**,* who brought you out of Egypt, out of the land of slavery.
>
> ³ "You shall have **no other gods** before me.
>
> ⁴ "You shall **not make for yourself an image** in the form of anything in heaven above or on the earth beneath or in the waters below.
>
> ⁵ You shall **not bow down** to them or worship them; **for I, the Lord your God, am a jealous God**, punishing the

children for the sin of the parents to the third and fourth generation of those who hate me,

⁶ but showing love to a thousand generations of those who love me and keep my commandments. (Exodus 20:2-6 NIV, emphasis mine)

Because of this God withdraw his presence from them. This is what sin does a gap between God and His people.

The people have replaced the true God with the "god of gold" or "the calf idol." Their act was a blatant rejection of God who rescued them from slavery in Egypt. God was ostracized by His own people replaced Him with "god of gold" that can't help them. The people made their own material god for themselves. This rebellion causes God to withdraw Himself from His own people.

Have we replaced God with "god of gold?" Have we created our own material gods that causes God's presence to distance from us? Have we created a gap by making our personal idols that dethroned Jesus from our heart? Remember, sin causes Jesus to withdraw His presence from us. The only way to close the gap is an authentic prayer of repentance in humility what Moses did when he acknowledges and identifies with the sins of his own people. For God's presence to return in our midst we must first return to God and turn away from idolatry or any form of idols we've created in our hearts, confess them and repent from them wholeheartedly. We must return to God for God to return to us. We must acknowledge Him the only true God Creator of heavens and earth, the God who rescued us from the claws of Satan and eternal damnation. We must acknowledge the only true God Jesus Christ who died for the forgiveness of our sins.

Jesus Christ is the only way to the heavenly Father. Jesus is the only one who can close the gap. Jesus is the way the truth and the life to the Father.

After Moses interceded for his own people and pleaded for God's grace, God changed His mind (Exo.33:12-13). God said, *"My presence will go with you, and I will give you rest"* (Exodus 33:14 NKJV). Prayer of repentance done in the spirit of humility always works. God listened to Moses' plea for His presence.

## "Humility and repentance pleases God a posture of the heart that always gets His attention."

### Francis Herras

*Humility and repentance pleases God a posture of the heart that always gets His attention.* This is your upward momentum! Moses' humble intercession closed the gap between God and His people. Prayer of repentance in humility is an aroma ascending to God's throne of Grace that draws Him closer to His people. When we turn our back from idolatry, it draws God's presence back in our lives.

Moses interceded for God's presence to go with them. As God's appointed leader leading God's people, he was not willing to move forward and take another step to the Promise Land without God's presence with them.

Moses pleaded for God's presence listen to him.

> ¹⁵ Then Moses said to him, "If *your Presence* does not go with us, do not send us up from here.
>
> ¹⁶ How will anyone know that you are pleased with me and with your people unless you *go with us? What else will distinguish me and your people* from all the other people on the face of the earth?" (Exodus 33:15-16 NIV).

For Moses God's presence means they are people favored by God and identified with God. God's presence is their distinguishing mark from other people on earth. It defines who they are and who their God is.

After God assured Moses of His presence going with them in the journey to the Promise Land, Moses proceeded to ask more from God. Moses asked the unthinkable. He asked something truly serious that could end his life. Moses asked God to show Himself to him. Moses was asking to see the Person of God. Meaning he wants to see God literally. Moses plea transitioned from God's presence to the Person of God. *For Moses God's manifest presence was not enough, he wants the Person of God.* But bear in mind the level of intimacy of the conversation between God and Moses. But why Moses asked God to show Himself? Here is why? Moses knew what is at stake—his identity, the people's identity and their nation. Moses has to be assured God is with Him all the way. He had to be assured not only of God's presence but more critically with God in Person working with Him and His people.

❦❦❦

# "For Moses God's manifest Presence was not enough, he wants the Person of God."

### Francis Herras

❦❦❦

Moses pleaded for the Person of God. Then Moses said, "Now *show me* your glory" (Exodus 33:18 NIV). In other words, Moses was saying, "Please God, show me Yourself." Or "Show Yourself to me."

God replied to Moses.

> ¹⁹ And the LORD said, "*I will cause all my goodness to pass in front of you*, and *I will proclaim my name, the LORD, in your presence.* I will have mercy on whom I will have mercy, and I will have compassion on whom I will have compassion.

> ²⁰ But," he said, "*you cannot see my face, for no one may see me and live.*"

> ²¹ Then the LORD said, "There is a place near me where you may stand on a rock.

> ²² When my glory passes by, I will put you in a cleft in the rock and cover you with my hand until I have passed by.

> ²³ Then I will remove my hand and *you will see my back*; but my face must not be seen." (Exodus 33:19-23 NIV)

*Identity and meaning is important.* For Moses knowing who you draw your identity and meaning from and why was extremely important. For Moses God's Presence defines him and the Hebrew people from the rest of the nations of the earth. For Moses God's Presence was essential to their identity. As a leader, Moses draws his personal identity from God which defines his leadership.

The Book of Exodus concludes with the glory of God hovering protectively over the Tabernacle and His people.

When Moses was done building the Tabernacle, God indwells it inside out. *"Then the glory of the Lord filled the Tabernacle" (Exodus. 40:34 NKJV).* God was pleased with Moses' work. God came and dwell upon the midst of His people. The people literally see the manifest presence of the glory of God through "the cloud" that covered the Tabernacle. "The glory of the Lord" filled the Tabernacle.

God was with His people. He tabernacle with them. He shows Himself up and assured His presence and ownership of them. God was gracious to show His glory among His people by dwelling in their midst.

The assurance of God's presence to the Israelites gives them peace, confidence, assurance, and direction. God Himself has been their company in their journey to the Promise Land. They were well preserved and protected by God. The cloud above the Tabernacle has become a form of God's communication with His people to let them know when to move and not to move in their journey to the Promise Land. When the cloud stays above the Tabernacle, the people stay foot but when the cloud is lifted up from the tent, it's God's sign it's time to move forward in their journey. *But why do they have to wait until the cloud of God's glory was lifted up before taking action to move forward?* The cloud was not only God's sign for them to move but it was likewise for their own safety—the preservation of their lives. No one can come near the Tent of Tabernacle when covered with the cloud let alone touch it or disassemble it to get ready to move for the journey. The only way for Moses and his people to get near the Tent of Tabernacle to dismantle it was when the cloud of God's glory is lifted otherwise many will perish.

God's timing was extremely important for the Israelites to follow for their own safety. Moses and his people have learned to embrace God's timing when to move forward and when to stay a foot. They've learned to follow God's divine direction pivotal to their journey. God knew the time and season and what lies ahead of them both good and evil. God's direction was crucial for the safety and accuracy as forge forward uncharted territory with God to have the Promise Land.

> "Whenever the cloud was taken up from above the tabernacle, the children of Israel would go onward in all their journeys. But if the cloud was not taken up, then they did not journey till the day that it was taken up" (Exodus 40:36-37 NKJV).

What was God saying to His people in terms of timing? Here is what God was telling them and us 21st Christian today:

"Just follow my direction, I got this."

"I am in charge."

"I've got you covered."

"I'm here."

"Be at peace I'm with you."

"Do not be afraid."

"Do what I say."

"Listen and follow me."

This is the view (perspective) from God everyone should know. This is the attitudes of humility that transform and leads to success in life—God's Promise Land for your life!

᠈᠈᠈

# ABOUT THE AUTHOR

Francis P. Herras is married to Evelyn for 28 years with four children. He and his family live in the City of Chestermere Lake in Alberta Canada.

Francis is a seasoned professional with over 36 years of work experience, with 15 years of management and leadership experience, including a high level position; with extensive experience in pastoral ministry and healthcare chaplaincy.

Francis is a Certified Elder Planning Counselor (CEIPS), a Certified Temperament Counselor (NCCA), holds a degree of Bachelor of Theology and double Master's degree in Pastoral Ministry and Missions and is now working on his doctoral degree in Clinical Christian Counseling.

Francis has a strong work ethic and is highly motivated, possessing strategic, analytical, and innovative thinking skills. He is a visionary. Francis consistently provides effective program and service delivery as well as responsible leadership of resources alignment with the organization's priorities, values, and mission.

Francis is a counselor, coach, mentor, trainer, and speaker. He helps unsatisfied *employees* build momentum to win in life so they can enjoy their work and meaningful lifestyle. He helps *families* sculpt their financial blueprint on achieving their financial goals through various financial, investments, insurances, education, mortgage, retirement, health plans and debt consolidation so they can save more to gain more. He offers *elderly consultancy* on retirement solutions, financial and planning issues, insurance issues and needs, aging and health issues, impact of an aging society, social, psychological and communication issues.

His passion is to educate people from various walks of life providing holistic care services through Christ-centered coaching, counseling, chaplaincy and consultancy to help them move forward carry out their God-given purpose in life. He aims to serve the hopeless, the hurting, frustrated, and those who have given up their dreams.

❧❧❧

**Forward Momentum Care Services**

*Information how you and your organization can avail Forward Momentum Services*

**For Free Workshop Registration Contact**

> **Francis Herras**
> Phone: 403-800-8580
> Email: fherras20@gmail.com

**Message from the Author:**

*"I help unsatisfied employees build momentum to win in life, so they can enjoy their work and meaningful lifestyle. I am like a train track for the journey of designing success blueprint at work."*

**The Mission of Forward Momentum Care Services**

**Care for Employees and Professionals**

> To help unsatisfied employees build momentum to win in life so they can enjoy their work and meaningful lifestyle.

**Care for Family**

> To help families sculpt their financial blueprint on achieving their financial goals through various financial, investments, insurances, education, mortgage, retirement, health plans and debt consolidation so they can save more to gain more.

**Care for Elderly**

> To offer elderly consultancy on retirement solutions, financial and planning issues, insurance issues and needs, aging and health issues, impact of an aging society, social, psychological and communication issues.

Forward Momentum offers care services that considers seriously the connection and interaction of the *spiritual, psychological (intellect, emotion, will) and physiological* aspects of the employees/clients into account when assessing, planning and carrying out necessary care plans needed by the clients to succeed in life and at work.

**Forward Momentum Offers ...**

*Coaching*— keynote speaking, training, workshop, webinars, etc
Churches
Corporate Business/Organizations
Personal and Professional Development
Financial Issues and Planning
Insurance Issues and Needs

*Counseling*— elder planning counseling, temperament counseling, faith base
Individual
Marriage
Family
Financial Issues and Planning
Insurance Issues and Needs
Soul Care

*Chaplaincy*— spiritual care, pastoral care, congregational care
Hospital
Nursing Homes
Corporate Business
Town Hall
Church/Congregation

*Consultancy*— Senior Care Services
Retirement Solution
Aging and Health
Social and Psychological Issues
Financial Issues and Planning
Communication and Other Issues (Fraud, Abuse, Ethics)
Impact of an Aging Society
Insurance Issues and Needs
The Role of an Elder Planning Counselor

# Forward Momentum the Art of Winning in Life

CPSIA information can be obtained
at www.ICGtesting.com
Printed in the USA
LVHW091906301118
598831LV00001B/4/P

9 781973 637813